D0418581

The Pocket Guide
to Cheese

As a freelance wine journalist, Barbara Ensrud writes a weekly column for the New York *Daily News* and regular columns for *Vogue, The Wine Spectator,* and many other newspapers and magazines. She is the author of *The Pocket Guide to Wine* and has also contributed to several best-selling wine books, including *The Joys of Wine* and *The New York Times Wine Book.* A member of the New York Wine Writers Circle and the International Wine and Food Society, Ms. Ensrud has traveled extensively in many vineyard regions of the world and frequently lectures on wine.

The Pocket Guide to CHEESE

Barbara Ensrud

FREDERICK MULLER LIMITED
LONDON

First published in Great Britain in 1981 by **Frederick Muller Limited,** London, NW2 6LE

ISBN: 0 584 95002 0

The Pocket Guide to Cheese
was produced and prepared by
Quarto Marketing Ltd.
212 Fifth Avenue, New York, NY 10010

Editors: John Smallwood and Wendy L. Ruoff
Editorial Research: Bill Logan
Designed by Ken Diamond and Elizabeth Fox
Maps by Randall Lieu
Illustrations by Dinah Lone and Susan Sykes
Design Assistant: Jack Donaghy
Copy Editor: Susan Newman

Printed and bound in the United States of America by Maple-Vail Group

CONTENTS

INTRODUCTION

When I began this little odyssey through cheesedom, my enthusiasm for fine cheese had already developed quite nicely, right alongside my interest in wine. In the course of many months of concentrated research and tasting, however, something happened. While I have long enjoyed the mystery and luxury presented by numerous European cheese boards during travels abroad, suddenly, in the midst of *this* intensive journey, I developed a passion for the stuff.

Where before I was content to enjoy cheese as an occasional snack or after dinner with a fine wine (the wine chosen first and *then* the cheese to accompany it), I now find myself hooked, unable even for a day to be without a goodly cache in my refrigerator. There *must* be an excellent Cheddar available at all times, a fine, nutty Gruyère or a log of *chèvre,* and something from the soft-ripened family, be it Münster, Rollot or L'Ami du Chambertin. These, of course, supplemented fairly frequently by the brief-lived glory of a perfectly ripened Brie or Camembert.

Such an unexpected love affair is a fate that could befall anyone who undertakes a similar journey through the world's cheeses. And I suspect that those who do so will likely end up as I have, with admiration for the grand diversity of existing cheeses, the patient and painstaking artistry that certain ones entail, and the triumph of cooperation between man and nature.

Cheese is one of humankind's oldest foodstuffs. It has nourished, soothed, and satisfied the deepest of physical hungers, resuscitated flagging energies, and filled and fulfilled sensuous yearnings since the dawn of civilization. A superb cheese, once experienced and savored, lingers in memory the same way an extraordinary wine does, its afterglow of flavor coming back to spark a longing for its like again.

It was Clifton Fadiman—epic (and Epicurean) worksmith—who coined the phrase that best describes cheese as "milk's leap to immortality." The legend of how cheese was discovered has an appropriately exotic and romantic ring to it. Thousands of years ago, it is told, an Asian nomad set out on a journey by horse or camel, transporting milk in a leather pouch made from a calf's stomach. After many hours of rhythmic jogging in the warm sun, the rider grew thirsty and when he looked inside his saddlebag, the milk had turned into curds. The substance was not bad, he must have decided, for from that moment on, cheese became an important way to preserve surplus milk.

Today we know that it is the enzyme "rennin," which comes from rennet, a substance in the lining of calves' stomachs, that causes the solids in milk to coagulate. Little Miss Muffet's curds and whey were in fact very fresh cheese in its earliest stage of transformation.

The basic principles for making natural cheeses are much the same today as they have been for hundreds of years, though many of the steps have been highly mechanized. Bacterial "starter" cultures are added to fresh or pasteurized milk, which increases the acidity to a certain point. Then rennet is added, rapidly bringing about the curdling or clotting of the milk, separating it from the watery whey. The curds are then stirred with large forks or cut into cubes and heated to various temperatures to solidify them further or develop the proper texture.

After the draining of the curd, procedures vary somewhat for the different cheese types. Fresh cheeses are barely cooked at all, so as to retain their moist, loose-curd texture. The curds of Swiss cheese are gathered up in cheesecloth and lifted, dripping copiously, out of the whey and put into molds. Cheddar is cooked longer to hasten drainage of the whey, and then it is milled or cut into blocks and turned continuously in a process known as "cheddaring." Finally, it is put into cloth-lined molds and firmly pressed into the close, dense, satiny texture for which it is noted. Ripening times for cheeses also vary. Some ripen quickly, within a few days or weeks of production; others are cured for months, or even years.

One final word: while we are fortunate to be able to get so many cheeses heretofore unavailable, I urge those who travel abroad to try local cheeses whenever they present themselves. Better yet, seek them out. You may discover something quite fantastic—more immediately exciting and personally gratifying than the discovery of a new star.

HOW TO USE THIS BOOK

The attempt with this volume has been to include the most important cheese classics, as well as certain newer cheeses—those of recent development and older cheeses that are nevertheless somewhat "new" to us through the advantages of modern transport.

The emphasis is on natural cheeses, and focuses more on authentic prototypes. Processed cheeses and imitations such as Swiss types produced outside of Switzerland, various semisoft cheeses, and countless blues get less attention for the most part (and less enthusiasm from me unless they are exceptionally well done). Imitation in the cheese world is profligate, though not necessarily to be denigrated, as a burgeoning world demand encourages it. Rarely, however, do the imitations match the originals for depth of character and complexity of flavor.

Most of the important cheeses included here are preceded by specifications designed to give a quick indication of the cheese's character, flavor, and appearance, denoting *origin, type, taste, appearance,* and *availability* in the world cheese market. Each cheese is indexed, and cross-references are given throughout the text. Cross references appear in SMALL CAPS.

This book is intended mainly as a guide to selecting and serving cheese for the consumer. For more detailed information on the technicalities of making cheeses and in-depth discussion of *types*, please see "Further Reading" on page 137.

◆ CLASSIFYING CHEESES ◆

Categorizing cheeses has always been somewhat problematical because many of their characteristics overlap while other characteristics make them entirely different from one another. Technical experts ˉand the cheese producers themselves tend to use terms that are arcane and convey very little to the consumer, who is, after all, primarily interested in flavor, appearance, and texture.

The most basic measure of the differences among cheeses is the degree of hardness, but categories such as hard, soft, and semi-soft are in many cases too broad to be of much use without further qualification. What I have tried to do here, under *type* in the specifications for each entry, is to use the term that best conveys the most distinctive characteristic of the cheese. Sometimes the chosen term will indeed refer to the degree of hardness, but at other times, the ripening method or type of rind or the origin of the milk is more indicative of character.

The method of production is important in certain cases, such as that of the *pasta filata* cheeses, where the curd is stretched and kneaded—a technique that is quite distinct from those used in the production of most other cheeses and the effect of which is immediately evident in the texture of Mozzarella, Provolone, or Caciocavallo. On the other hand, the most notable aspect of cheeses like Livarot or Liederkranz is their pungency of odor. Therefore, the term 'strong-smelling' may be used to type cheeses that might also be described as 'soft-ripened' or 'washed-rind' cheeses.

Despite the effort to categorize each cheese by its most salient feature, there are some overlaps that may be confusing, and certain cheeses will fall within two or more categories. Monastery cheeses, such as Port Salut, are generally semi-soft, but very ripe Münster could certainly be listed among the strong-smelling.

For those who wonder how I arrived at this particular system of classification (which doesn't differ radically from others except in a few instances), let me say that it is largely arbitrary but is based on conversations with some of the country's leading cheese vendors. I recognize that there are points to be made for other approaches, but it seemed burdensome to have too many categories and those I've used seemed to be the most useful for consumers. Following is an explanation of each category I've used under the *type* specification, together with "Buying and Storing Tips" and "Serving Tips" for each category.

Hard
(SUB-TYPE: *Grana*)

The hard cheeses, the prototype of which is Italy's Parmigiano-Reggiano, are primarily used for grating. The word for such cheeses in Italian is *grana,* which means "grain" and denotes the grainy texture that results from long aging. They are also known, technically, as cooked, pressed cheeses because the curd is heated to between 125° and 140°F, then pressed into close-textured firmness. Most grating cheeses must be aged at least two years; four are better, and a few cheeses, such as Saanen or Sapsago, receive six or seven years. Twenty years' ripening is not unheard of, but it is rare, especially today.

The hard cheeses include Saanen, Sapsago, and Sbrinz of Switzerland; Parmigiano, Grana Padano, and Pecorino Romano of Italy; and Kefalotyri of Greece. Certain cheeses usually classed as semi-firm become harder with additional age and similarly suitable for grating. Among these are Aged Asiago, Dry California Jack, and Aged Gouda.

♦ **Buying and Storing Tips:** Hard cheeses obviously age well, but they should *not* be dried out, have cracked rinds, be too grainy or mealy in texture, or show heavy concentrations of white crystals. Nor should they be overly salty or bitter—try to sample before buying. *Parmigiano-Reggiano* is a strictly controlled cheese name and all authentic versions have it stencilled on the rind. The most flavorful seasoning comes from cheese you grate yourself; pre-grated cheese, even from specialty shops that use only the finest grades, loses its distinctiveness in a matter of hours. Whole cheeses of this sort, on the other hand, keep extremely well if securely wrapped in wax paper or foil and refrigerated or stored in a cool place.

♦ **Serving Tips:** Young versions of many grating cheeses (Parmigiano, Grana, Sbrinz) are closer to semi-firm than hard in texture and make excellent eating cheeses, accompanied by fresh fruit and sturdy red wines like Barolo, Barbaresco, Barbera, or Sfursat.

Semi-Firm
(SUB-TYPES: *Swiss, Cheddar*)

This broad category includes cooked, pressed cheeses, rindless or with natural rinds, that are firm but not hard or brittle in texture. They may be close-textured, smooth, and slightly flaky like the Cheddars, Double Gloucester, French Cantel, Edam, Mimolette, or Aged Gouda; somewhat more open-textured like Cheshire or Lancashire; or very open like the "holey" cheeses, Swiss Emmentaler, Gruyère, Beaufort, Jarlsberg, Danbo, Samsoe, or Kanburra. The holes in cheese are formed by gases released during ripening.

Most cheeses of this category come in large, heavy wheels, or cylinders that weigh anywhere from 20 to 120 pounds. The numerous imitators of Cheddar and Swiss Emmentaler comprise much of this category, but there are other semi-firm cheeses with an individual character of their own, such as Fontina Val d'Aosta.

♦ **Buying and Storing Tips:** Beware of cracked rinds, a dried-out appearance, or an overly crumbly texture. Always taste the cheese if possible and avoid any cheeses that are bitter or rancid. Cheddars or Cheddar-relatives that are darker near the rind or at cut edges may not have been properly stored and may have hardened or dried out. Be specific about the origin of Cheddar (English, Farmhouse, New York, Oregon, Canadian) and of Swiss from Switzerland. The words "Imported Swiss" on the label do not automatically mean that the cheese was made in Switzerland—it may just as well have come from Finland, Austria, or Australia.

A sign of quality and maturity for Swiss-style cheeses is "weeping eyes"—the holes glisten with butterfat. The number of holes vary in number (Appenzell has few, Gruyère has many) and size (as small as peas or as large as walnuts), but they should be typical for the particular cheese as it is described in the Cheese Guide. Pre-cut, pre-packaged cheeses, such as those found in supermarkets, are convenient but have less flavor and character than portions freshly cut from whole cheeses. Semi-firm cheeses will keep very well for several weeks or longer if wrapped in plastic and refrigerated.

♦ **Serving Tips:** The semi-firm cheeses make fine after-dinner cheeses, especially in the company of cheeses with contrasting flavors or textures. They go well with balanced red wines such as Bordeaux, Cabernet Sauvignon, or Rioja. They are also fine for snacks or picnics with fresh fruit and lighter wines, cider, beer, or ale.

Semi-Soft
(SUB-TYPE: *Monastery*)

This category, too, comprises a large group, embracing many of the so-called bland and buttery cheeses, such as Gouda, Bel Paese, Morbier, most Fontinas, Havarti, Samsoe, and the

Danish "bo" cheeses (Tybo, Fynbo, Maribo), Taleggio, and spiced cheeses such as Leyden or Nökkelost. They do tend to be mild-flavored and are higher in moisture content, with a smooth, sliceable texture that makes them very popular in sandwiches or for snacks.

Cheeses of the sub-type *monastery* (sometimes known as Trappist cheeses) are a little more complicated. The prototypes—Alsatian Münster, Swiss Tête de Moine, French Port-Salut—were indeed developed by Trappist monks in monasteries, some as far back as the Middle Ages. Most semi-soft cheeses, including many named in the preceding paragraph, as well as German Tilsit, French Saint-Paulin, American Brick, Danish Esrom, Canadian Oka, and others, derive from the early monastery types. Some have surface-ripened, washed rinds that continue ripening over time. Such cheeses as Pont-l'Evêque, Robiola Introbio, and Reblochon can become quite soft and develop a pungent flavor and aroma.

♦ **Buying and Storing Tips:** Semi-soft cheeses generally keep well for several weeks or longer if properly wrapped and refrigerated. The texture should be moist and smooth. With monastery types, especially those of the washed-rind variety, beware of rank odor, gummy rinds, sticky or discolored paper, and cheeses that have shrunk away from the container or wrapper.

♦ **Serving Tips:** Semi-soft cheeses make excellent snack or sandwich cheeses: the stronger-flavored monastery types are superb for cheese boards and can take sturdy, full-bodied red wines or crisp Alsace Rieslings.

Soft-Ripened
(SUB-TYPES: *Bloomy rind, Washed rind*)

Surface-ripened cheeses are sprayed with or exposed to molds that cause them to ripen from the rind inward. The rinds are of two types: thin, white crusts that develop a velvety, white "bloom," known as bloomy rinds, and found on Brie, Camembert, or Carré de l'Est; and orange-hued "washed" rinds that are treated or cured with various solutions of brine, wine and spices, beer, or grape brandy such as Marc de Bourgogne. The soft-ripened cheeses have either a semi-soft consistency to begin with, or, like Brie, Camembert, or Coulommiers, firm, chalky centers that become soft and creamy as they ripen. Some of the soft-ripened cheeses fall into other categories as well. Many monastery and strong-smelling cheeses, such as Münster, Pont l'Evêque, Livarot, and Maroilles, also have washed rinds. Most of the double and triple creams such as Boursault, Brillat-Savarin, Chaource, and Caprice des Dieux, have downy white rinds.

The soft-ripened varieties are among the most delectable and popular of cheeses and some are capable of great nuance and complexity. Their lives are short, but often glorious. They ripen quickly and at their peak may last only a day or two, sometimes less, then tend to become ammoniated or rank. Factory-made versions (labeled *laitier* in France) generally have a somewhat longer life and more uniform consistency but are less distinctive in character.

♦ **Buying and Storing Tips**: Soft-ripened cheeses are considered ripe when they are plump within the rind, yielding, yet slightly springy to the touch. Once cut, they will not ripen further to any noticeable degree. It is necessary, then, to note carefully the texture of pre-cut Brie. For instance, if the center has a caky white line, the cheese may be quite good, but it is not fully ripe. Watch out for hardened or gummy rinds, darkened color, ammoniated aromas, or excessive runniness —these are sure indications that the cheese is past its prime.

Washed-rind cheeses should not have rank or "barnyardy" aromas. Avoid those with gummy rinds or those that are shrunken or misshapen.

Soft-ripened cheeses keep a short time once they are fully ripe. Wrap them in plastic and refrigerate in the vegetable crisper.

♦ **Serving Tips**: Soft-ripened cheeses are top choices for after dinner, especially as a contrast to blues, semi-firm cheeses, or *chèvres*. Remove them from the refrigerator two to three hours before serving. The strong odors of the washed-rind varieties will dissipate somewhat if they are allowed to stand in a well-circulated atmosphere. The rinds are edible, but eating them is a matter of preference and they should be trimmed if they are overly strong.

Blue Vein

The blue-veined cheeses, marbled with bluish-green mold, are among the most intense and strong-flavored cheeses of all and include some of the most famous names in cheese— Roquefort, Stilton, Gorgonzola. Usually made from cow's milk (Roquefort is made from ewe's milk), they originally developed their mottled character spontaneously from spores of mold in the atmosphere where they were cured. Today nothing is left to chance, and most blue cheeses are innoculated or sprinkled with spores of *Penicillium glaucum* or *Penicillium roqueforti,* then skewered with holes to admit air, which encourages the mold. Most blues are dead white or pale ivory between the pockets or streaks of bluish (sometimes greenish) mold. The exception is Blue Cheshire, which is a rich orange-gold. The veining may be light in a young cheese and become more dense with age.

The classic blues have been imitated by almost every cheese-producing country in the world. The greatest successes are modeled after Gorgonzola, piquant in flavor but slightly milder and similarly creamy in texture. Stilton and Roquefort, however, are still without rival. Other fine blues are the French Blue de Bresse, Pipo Crem', and Bleu d'Auvergne; Danablu of Denmark; Oregon Blue and Maytag Blue of the United States; and Queso de Cabrales of Spain.

♦ **Buying and Storing Tips:** Blue cheeses vary from piquant and creamy to sharp and tangy. Some have a faint bitterness that is entirely characteristic. It is always best to sample before you buy to see if the taste is what you want. That is something you cannot do with pre-wrapped portions, so try to buy from stores where cheeses are sold in bulk. Good specimens should not be overly salty, bitter, or dried out. Blue cheeses keep very well for a few weeks if they are securely wrapped in plastic and refrigerated. Large portions keep much longer. Whole Stiltons or Roqueforts wrapped in damp cloth will keep for months if portions are cut as they are needed and the cheese is carefully re-wrapped.

♦ **Serving Tips:** Use a very sharp knife or a cheese wire for cutting blues so that they don't crumble. Wheels such as Stilton or Roquefort should be cut in half horizontally and then in wedges, starting at the top and moving down through the cheese in layers about two inches thick. Blues make an excellent contrast to other cheeses on the cheese board, but they are also superb with fresh apples, pears, or grapes and a sweet wine such as Sauterne, late-harvest Riesling, or Port.

Goat or Sheep
(SUB-TYPE: *Chèvre*)

Ewes and goats give less milk than cows, but it is higher in fat and protein and richer and more concentrated in flavor. Both milks yield cheeses of a sharp, sometimes intense character. They are often described as having a sheepy or goaty tang that immediately sets them apart from cow's milk cheeses. Today goat's and sheep's milks are frequently mixed with cow's milk or with each other (which may be indicated by the term *mélange de lait* on some French cheeses. The addition of cow's milk makes these cheeses milder and, in the case of *chèvres,* creamier. Sheep cheeses range from semi-soft to very hard in texture, depending upon age, and the older ones are often used for grating. Goat cheese, which is generally ripened for shorter periods, is moist and smooth.

The sub-type *chèvres* is commonly used for goat's milk cheeses in France and there are dozens of them that come in various small shapes (see *Chèvres,* p. 37). The phrase *pur chèvre* (also the generic term) supposedly means that the cheese is made from 100% goat's milk, but there is no law to enforce this as yet. Increasingly, goat's milk is mixed with cow's milk because the latter is so much more abundant and is available year-round.

Goat and sheep cheeses are most widely produced in France, Italy, Spain, Greece, central Europe, and the Middle East. Roquefort is the most famous cheese made from ewe's milk (see Blue Vein). Other famous ones are Pecorino

Romano, Fiore Sardo, and the Caciottas of Italy; Corsican Venaco; Spanish Manchego; Balkan Kashkaval. The most famous—and most widely imitated—goat cheese is Greek Feta. It is also one of the world's oldest and now commonly includes cow's milk

♦ **Buying and Storing Tips:** Taste before buying, if possible, since these cheeses generally have a pronounced flavor and vary seasonally, with the best usually available from early autumn to May. Very ripe *chèvres* may be potent and sharp, especially if the rind has toughened. The French often prefer them this way. *Chèvres* have a relatively brief life but may keep up to two weeks if carefully wrapped and refrigerated, although they lose moisture and become sharper with age. Feta should be stored in a bath of salty or plain water to keep it moist; a milk bath will mitigate the saltiness. Sheep cheeses generally keep very well for long periods if they are not allowed to dry out.

♦ **Serving Tips:** The extra punch of flavor in sheep and goat cheeses makes them highly desirable as after-dinner cheeses providing vivid flavor contrasts to other types. Dry, fruity white wines, mature Bordeaux or Burgundy, and Port make excellent accompaniments.

Pasta Filata

Pasta filata are the stretched-curd cheeses of Italy and include Mozzarella, Provolone, Scamorze, Caciocavallo, and others. The term means "spun paste" and refers to the method of bathing the curd in hot whey, then kneading and stretching it to the desired consistency. They are also sometimes called "plastic curd" cheeses. The pliable texture, ranging from the softness of fresh mozzarella to the firm smoothness of Provolone or Caciocavallo, should not be rubbery or tough.

♦ **Buying and Storing Tips:** Fresh mozzarella is fragile and should be bought as fresh as possible and consumed within a day or two. Firmer cheeses last a good deal longer, up to several weeks or even months for aged Provolone, but they must be carefully wrapped or they will dry out and harden.

♦ **Serving Tips:** Mozzarella and Provolone are widely used in cooking, but also for snacking and in sandwiches or salads. Lightly smoked versions and Scamorze can be delicious with light red or white wines. Aged Provolone is sharp and assertive and calls for sturdy reds.

Double and Triple Creams

These are cow's milk cheeses enriched with cream. Double creams must have at least 60% fat, triple creams, 75%. They may be fresh, like Boursin, or have bloomy white rinds, like L'Explorateur, Chaource, and Gratte Paille. Their alluring richness and seductive creaminess completely beguile beginning cheeselovers, but experienced turophiles find them irresistible as well.

♦ **Buying and Storing Tips:** These cheeses should be plump and full inside the rind or wrapping and should not be hard or discolored. They will keep up to a week if wrapped in plastic and refrigerated.

♦ **Serving Tips:** Double and Triple Creams are often substituted for dessert, served with ripe pears, plums, or peaches; and lightly sweet Rieslings, Sauternes, Champagnes, or fruity red wines.

Fresh

The fresh cheeses are uncooked and unripened. They include Pot Cheeses, Cottage Cheese, Cream Cheese, Stracchino, Ricotta, Gervais, and others. Some are rich and creamy (fresh double cream). They are commonly mild and very moist, with a pleasantly sourish tang or tartness; they should not be overly acidic, nor should they be bitter.

♦ **Buying and Storing Tips:** Fresh cheeses, it should go without saying, should be purchased as fresh as possible. They are fragile and rarely keep beyond a week or ten days—less for imported ones such as Ricotta, Stracchino, Crescenza, or the fresh Robiolas. Fresh double creams, such as Boursin, have longer life. They should be securely wrapped or kept in tightly capped containers and refrigerated.

♦ **Serving Tips:** Fresh cheeses are versatile choices for breakfast, lunch, and snacks, and are often topped with fresh berries or preserved fruit. They may also be mixed with herbs or other flavorings.

Strong-Smelling

The chief feature of cheeses in this group, composed mainly of the washed-rind varieties, announces itself boldly or even overpoweringly. The word "Limburger" is virtually synonymous with pungency of aroma. Limburger's cohorts and rivals are many: Liederkranz, Livarot, Maroilles, Handkäse, Schloss, Hervé, Romadur. Their rinds all are washed or smeared with solutions that contribute to their *odeur puissant*, "stinky odor." Very ripe Münster or Pont l'Evêque could be included here also.

Though not for the faint-hearted, these cheeses need no apologists. Their fans are ardently enthusiastic and eagerly dive through the thick curtain of aroma to the delights of the cheese within. "What cognac is to wine," said one notable cheese-monger, "the washed rinds are to cheese." Oftentimes, their bark is worse than their bite; the assertive character of the cheese itself is surprisingly delicious, even to the uninitiated—intensely savory but milder than the aroma would intimate. For devotées, however, the stronger the better.

♦ **Buying and Storing Tips**: These cheeses will be fresh and resiliently plump inside the rind when ripe or nearly so. Underripe cheeses will be slightly firm to the touch. Hardened rinds, shrunken or mis-shapen cheeses, and ammoniated flavors indicate overripeness. Wiping the rind with a damp cloth or salty water will remove some of the odor and slow ripening a bit, but these cheeses must be well-wrapped to keep them from overpowering everything in their environment. If a smelly cheese is left uncovered for a few hours before serving, some of its odor will dissipate—but be sure the area is well-ventilated. Cover it with a cheese bell to contain the aroma.

♦ **Serving Tips**: Serve strong-smelling cheese separately from other cheeses (not on the same board or tray) so as not to overpower the more delicate types. It is also advisable to provide a separate serving knife. Assertive, full-bodied wines, such as Alsace Riesling Reserve or robust reds, are called for.

Whey

Whey cheeses are those made from the watery, white, or yellowish liquid that separates from the curds when milk and rennet are heated together. Italian Ricotta is a fresh whey cheese. Norwegian Gjetost, which is caramel-colored and somewhat sweet in taste, is a cooked whey cheese.

♦ **Buying and Storing Tips**: Ricotta is very perishable and is best when very fresh. It will keep up to five or six days, but then begins to sour or become moldy. Gjetost will keep extremely well for several weeks or more if it is securely wrapped in foil or plastic and refrigerated.

♦ **Serving Tips**: See Ricotta page 71 and Gjetost page 96.

Processed

Processed cheeses are made by mixing natural cheeses with emulsifiers, additives, and sometimes special flavorings to give them longer shelf life. Most are soft to semi-soft and rather elastic in texture, with mild flavors and not much character. They are designed to appeal to a wide audience, which in fact they do; tremendous quantities are sold in Europe and the United States. American processed cheeses are mostly Cheddar-based, while European ones make use of surplus Emmental or Gruyère. Some of the best-known brands are La Vache Qui Rit, Neufchâtel, Swiss Knight, Velveeta, Gourmandise, Kavli, Reybier, and Reybino.

♦ **Buying and Storing Tips**: Most processed cheeses are foil-wrapped and it is not possible to tell if they are fresh. They last very well, however, and are generally reliable when purchased from reputable marketers.

♦ **Serving Tips**: Processed cheeses are mostly used for snacks.

◆ Nutrition in Popular Cheeses ◆

CHEESE TYPE	Fat (grams/oz)	Protein (grams/oz)	Calories (per oz)
Speisequark (no-fat)	0	3.9	21
Cottage Cheese (1% fat)	0.3	3.5	20
Cottage Cheese (creamed)	1.2	3.8	30
Danbo (10% fat)	1.6	9.8	55
Ricotta (part skim)	2.5	3.5	43
Ricotta	4.0	3.6	54
Mozzarella (part skim)	4.5	6.9	72
Edam	5.7	7.7	87
Feta	6.0	4.0	74
Mozzarella	6.1	5.4	79
Parmesan	7.3	10.1	111
Provolone	7.3	7.4	98
Gouda	7.7	7.0	100
Limburger	7.7	5.7	93
Brie	7.8	5.8	94
Emmental	7.8	7.7	104
Port du Salut	7.9	6.7	99
Blue	8.5	6.0	103
Monterey	8.5	6.8	105
Cheshire	8.6	6.5	108
Fontina	8.7	7.2	109
Roquefort	8.7	6.1	105
Gruyère	8.9	8.1	115
Cheddar	9.1	7.0	112
Cream	9.9	2.1	99

Fat in cheese is a complicated and confusing subject. A figure of 45% fat IDM on a cheese label refers to the percentage of fat "in dry matter" only, that is, the dry solids excluding water. Most cheeses on the average consist of 30 to 70 percent moisture (or water). Thus in certain instances high moisture cheeses such as Brie or Camembert may contain considerably less fat than the 45 percent figure would indicate.

The fat content of cheese depends upon the fat in the milk used to make it. But diet-conscious folk should be aware that so-called skimmed milk cheese may not be lower in fat in the end because cream is often added for texture and flavor. It is the fat in the final cheese that counts. Jarlsberg, for example, is made of partially skimmed milk, yet the final cheese contains 47 percent fat IDM, because U.S. standards require that minimum.

AUSTRALIA & NEW ZEALAND

ike other former British colonies, Australia and New Zealand began to manufacture cheeses in imitation of the mother country during the nineteenth century. Cheddars were, and still are, the chief variety, although both countries now produce very creditable versions of the world's most popular cheeses, from Swiss and Gouda to Limburger and Gorgonzola.

Cows and sheep alike flourish on the plains of southern Australia and the lush mountain valleys of New Zealand, but cheese is made primarily from cow's milk. Both countries have strong cheese industries, regulated by national boards with high quality standards and incentives for innovation. To date there are no extraordinary new creations, but the cheeses are of consistent quality and often offer good value.

◆

Cheese Guide

BLUE VEIN, NEW ZEALAND
A creamy blue cheese made from cow's milk in the soft spreadable style of Danablu from Denmark.

CHEDDAR, AUSTRALIAN

ORIGIN	*southern Australia/cow's milk*
TYPE	*Cheddar/50% fat*
TASTE	*mild to sharp*
APPEARANCE	*Cheddar-like but varies in color and firmness*
AVAILABILITY	*general export*

Cheddar is widely produced in many parts of southern Australia. Some of the best comes from the Margaret River region in the West. Mild Cheddar is aged about three months, mature six to twelve months, and vintage Cheddar up to two years. Australians also like their Cheddars spiced up a bit, and many of them are flavored with garlic, cumin, bacon, or nuts.

Most medium-bodied red wines go well with these Cheddars, but they provide a good opportunity to try indigenous reds like Shiraz or Cabernet.

CHEDDAR, NEW ZEALAND

Quota restrictions limit the export of New Zealand Cheddars for the most part, though some reaches the United States where it is sold as Cheddar or Colby. It is mild, not especially interesting, but very inexpensive and acceptable as a snack cheese.

In New Zealand respectable versions of English-style Cheddars are made, including Cheshires, Gloucesters, Wensleydale, and others, but they are not exported to the United States.

CHEEDAM

ORIGIN	*Australia/cow's milk*
TYPE	*Cheddar/45% fat*
TASTE	*mild*
APPEARANCE	*semi-firm, pale yellow interior; sold in cylinders or blocks*
AVAILABILITY	*limited export*

A very popular "invented" cheese, developed as a cross between Cheddar and Edam. Much of it is exported to Japan, where mild cheeses are prized. Light fruity red wines or beer are suitable to drink with this cheese.

EGMONT

A relatively new cheese developed in New Zealand as a cross between Cheddar and Gouda. Egmont is also popular in Japan, but will soon be more widely exported. A mild cheese, it is best accompanied by light, fruity wines.

KANBURRA

An Australian Swiss-style cheese, very similar in flavor to good Norwegian Jarlsberg. Mild but appealing and inexpensive, Kanburra is increasingly exported. Its principal use is with snacks, light red wines or beer.

MACZOLA

An Australian version of Italian Gorgonzola, smaller in size and lower in fat than the original.

◆◆◆

BRITISH ISLES

The wholesome and satisfying goodness of fine English Cheddar has made it one of the world's most widely imitated cheeses. Like most originals, however, it remains in a class by itself. But it is only one—though perhaps the most famous—of Britain's "magnificent nine," a group that includes the mighty Stilton (contender with Roquefort and Brie for the world title, "king of cheeses"), as well as Cheshire, Lancashire, Wensleydale, and others.

The British love their own cheeses and of the nearly 200,000 tons produced annually, fewer than five percent are exported. The sight of a squatty cylinder of Stilton, with its wrinkled, crusty, brownish rind and creamy, blue-veined interior, is enough to set a Britisher's palate watering—especially if there is the prospect of pairing it with its classic partner, a glass of well-matured Port.

Cheese of one sort or another has been made in England for nearly 2,000 years. Farmhouse Cheddar is one of the oldest. Farmers of the Middle Ages made Cheddar; by Elizabethan times it was frequently cited in the literature of the day. Probably it tasted not unlike the Cheddars manufactured today, although the distinction is still drawn between what is known as "factory Cheddar" and traditional Farmhouse Cheddar, with its subtle depth and long, clean aftertaste of richness.

Early farmers made "New Milk Cheese" or "Morning Cheese" from the morning's whole milk mixed with the rich cream skimmed from the previous evening's milk. The resultant golden yellow cheese was thought to be the finest in England. For their own use, the farmers made a skimmed-milk cheese—hard, friable, and whitish—from the evening's leftover milk.

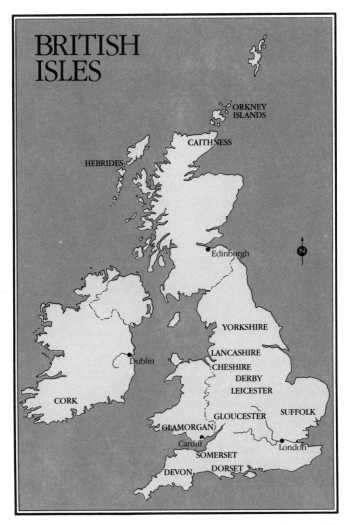

England's cheeses go back much farther than the Middle Ages, however; Roman legions posted in County Cheshire no doubt enjoyed an early version of salty, crumbly Cheshire cheese, thought to be England's oldest. Legend claims that the Roman legions built the wall around Chester, the capital of Cheshire County, to protect the city's cheese industry. English cheeses, although it is not known for sure which ones, very probably were sold at the *velabrium,* or dairy market, of ancient Rome.

Most of the cheeses of early Europe were made by dairymaids, the strong and sturdy wives and daughters of farmers. They were responsible for the process and often saw the milk through its entire journey from cow's udder to ripened cheese. Once rennet had been added to the milk in the cheese vat and the curds and whey separated, the dairymaid would scoop out the curds and place them in the primitive press. But first, since it was important that the curds be as dry as possible and mechanical presses were as yet unheard of, she would pre-press them by hand, often climbing on the lid of the cheese basket to apply her full body weight, whence the old English saying, "The bigger the maid, the better the cheese."

In the seventeenth century, cheese-making began to move off the farmstead and into the first dairy cooperatives. Farmers sent their milk to a central dairy where it was processed into cheese. Gradually, technical improvements and more efficient methods of production were developed. In the nineteenth century, for example, a cheese-maker named Joseph Harding helped relieve the milkmaids' burden when he standardized the "cheddaring" process. Under his system, still in use today, the curd is cut into blocks, turned, and folded at a temperature of 90°F to enhance the release of moisture. This procedure results in the tender texture for which British Cheddars are noted.

In spite of the increase in factory productivity, however, farmhouse cheeses are still made today on the farms that dot the meadows and moors of Somerset, Devonshire, Dorset, Cheshire, and Lancashire, although their number has dwindled from 1500 in 1939 to only 50 today. The appellation Farmhouse Cheese is rigidly controlled under quality standards set by the Farmhouse Cheese Association of England. Only a rough dozen or so British cheeses survive today, most named for the county or town where they originated or were first marketed. Cheeses are also made in Scotland and Ireland. Blarney is Ireland's answer to Swiss; Dunlop is Scottish Cheddar. Only four varieties are farm-produced: Cheddar, Cheshire, Blue Cheshire, and Lancashire, all of which are exported in very limited quantities. Farmhouse cheeses were first exported only to the west coast of the United States but now are available (to limited extent) in the East, mainly in New York, Boston, and a few specialty shops elsewhere.

◆

Cheese Guide

BLARNEY

ORIGIN	*Ireland/cow's milk*
TYPE	*semi-firm, Swiss/48% fat*
TASTE	*mild, buttery*
APPEARANCE	*bright yellow interior with numerous eyes; sold in red paraffin-rind wheels*
AVAILABILITY	*limited export*

A Swiss-style cheese, Blarney is one of the few cheeses still made in Ireland. Although it has Swiss-like holes and a golden color similar to Emmentaler's, it is milder and more buttery in texture and taste. It is rarely seen outside Ireland, although some is exported.

CABOC

ORIGIN *Scotland/cow's milk*
TYPE *double cream/62% fat*
TASTE *nutty, slightly sourish*
APPEARANCE *4-inch cylinder covered with oatmeal*
AVAILABILITY *domestic only*

This relatively new Scottish cheese holds the distinction of being one of the few double creams produced in the United Kingdom. Its outer coating of oatmeal gives it a somewhat nut-like flavor.

CAERPHILLY

ORIGIN *Wales/cow's milk*
TYPE *semi-firm/48% fat*
TASTE *mild, fresh, buttermilk-like tang*
APPEARANCE *sold in low cylinders or blocks; white interior with a smooth, moist, moderately firm texture*
AVAILABILITY *general export*

Welsh Caerphilly, named for the village in Wales where it was first made, is a young, fresh cheese popular with Welsh miners for its mild, easily digestible properties. It requires a much shorter aging period than traditional English Cheddar and for that reason was taken up by Cheddar makers in Somerset, for whom it has proven a lucrative sidelight. Cheddar is expensive and time-consuming to make; Caerphilly is cheap and quickly sold, ready for eating within a few weeks. Once made exclusively on farms in Wales, it is no longer made there but is produced in creameries, for the most part in Somerset.

As it ages, Caerphilly's mild tartness gets sharper and in England is considered past its prime after only a few weeks. For this reason, it should be bought fresh and eaten fairly quickly, especially when purchased outside Britain. Wrapping it in a damp cloth helps preserve its flavor. In an over-ripe state it is too salty and will have lost its sought-after mildness.

Caerphilly is delicious with fresh dark bread; celery, radishes, or other *crudités;* and salad. And it is well-suited to ale, dry, fruity white wines, or rosé.

CAITHNESS

A soft, high-fat Scottish cheese made in northern Scotland and rarely seen outside its homeland.

CHEDDAR

ORIGIN *Somerset/cow's milk*
TYPE *semi-firm, Cheddar/48% fat*
TASTE *distinctively rich and nutty with a clean, lingering finish*
APPEARANCE *50- to 60-pound cylinders or blocks; semi-firm, close-textured, ivory yellow to amber interior*
AVAILABILITY *general export*

Cheddar, the most widely imitated cheese in the world, was first made in southwestern England near the village of Cheddar in the Mendip Hills of Somerset County. English Cheddar is made both in farmhouse and factory. Many people think that there is no other cheese so wholesomely satisfying as genuine Farmhouse Cheddar. Certainly it is the highest-quality Cheddar, particularly that portion that is still made from fresh, unpasteurized milk. At one time the milk for Cheddar came only from Shorthorn cattle, but today most of it is provided by Friesians, along with other breeds.

The best and most highly prized Cheddar is made between May and October, when the milk is at its most flavorful because the cows are feeding on fresh grass. Winter Cheddar is richer and, because the cows feed on hay and other dried grains, higher in fat content. Farmhouse cheeses are graded on appearance, body, texture, and flavor, with Superfine as the highest grade, followed by Fine, Graded, and No-grade.

Only 26 farms now produce genuine Farmhouse Cheddar. Most English Cheddar now is made in the creamery (or factory) and therefore is more plentiful. Creamery Cheddar is very good, although it is made from various milks year 'round and doesn't have quite the incisive distinction and individuality of Farmhouse. But it is more uniform, if somewhat blander, in flavor and is more widely available.

Cheddar is of two kinds: mild and mature. A mild Cheddar, aged up to eight months, is mellow rather than sharp and has a clean, wholesome aftertaste. It is fine with bread and sweet butter, a medium-bodied red wine or full-bodied ale, and perhaps apples or pears. A mature Cheddar, aged over nine months and sometimes as long as two years, is rich, savory, and full-flavored with a lingering aftertaste, but without the bitterness of many imitative Cheddars. A good English Cheddar stands by itself at the end of a meal, a noble companion for well-aged Burgundy or a good Ruby Port. Cheddar melts well and is frequently used for Welsh rarebit in English pubs and grills.

The availability of English Cheddar in the United States is severely limited by American import quotas designed to protect domestic Cheddar production. However, specialty cheese shops on the east and west coasts consistently stock small quantities, including genuine Farmhouse Cheddar.

Ploughman's Lunch

Probably the most traditional way of serving English Cheddar is in Ploughman's Lunch, a lunchtime feature of most pubs in England. The ingredients are simple and must be fresh: a hunk of crusty bread, a piece of Cheddar, and perhaps some pickle, yet its delights prove that good ingredients need little adornment. The one accompaniment that no Englishman would forego, however, is a pint of bitter beer, which many would argue is the best companion for Cheddar at any time.

CHESHIRE

ORIGIN *Cheshire/cow's milk*
TYPE *semi-firm/48% fat*
TASTE *mild, creamy, salty*
APPEARANCE *pale yellow (White Cheshire), apricot (Red Cheshire), or blue-veined (Blue Cheshire) interiors; loosely textured and crumbly; sold in large cylinders or bricks*
AVAILABILITY *general export; Farmhouse Cheshire: limited export*

There are three types of Cheshire: Red, White, and Blue. The White and the Red are alike in flavor and texture, but Red Cheshire is colored with natural vegetable dye from the seeds of the annatto tree. Both have a mild but rich and appealing lactic flavor. Blue Cheshire is considered a great delicacy; it is richer, rarer, and more expensive than Red or White Cheshire.

Cheshire is one of England's most famous cheeses and its praises have been sung by the English literati, including Samuel Johnson. He and his cohorts were wont to sit about in a famous inn of the day, Ye Olde Cheshire Cheese on Fleet Street in London, happily sipping beer and ale and eating Cheshire cheese.

Red and White Cheshires are among the younger cheeses, ripening within a few weeks. If too old, they may turn bitter, although they are seldom aged longer than eight weeks in modern factory production. These "medium-ripened" Cheshires are remarkably consistent in quality, though not as delightful as the longer-ripened farmhouse variety. Farmhouse Cheshire, relatively rare, is richer and sometimes more intensely flavored than Cheddar; made during July and August from the richest milks of the year, it is aged eight to ten months.

Red and White Cheshires have long been considered ideal for Welsh rarebit and for the prototype of the grilled cheese sandwich. One seventeenth-century knight of the realm described Cheshire as a "quick, fat, well-tasted cheese to serve upon a piece of toast." Both versions are equally good served plain or with bread and butter or sliced tomatoes, and accompanied by beer and light red or dry white wines.

Blue Cheshire originated spontaneously when blue mold (*Penicillium glaucum*) developed on certain cheeses as they aged in the cellar. The first Blue Cheshires were considered spoiled and inedible, although they were sometimes used externally as ointments. When Yorkshire miners discovered that the rich, creamy, Cheshire taste was intensified by the blue mold, its distinctiveness soon became highly prized among cheese lovers. The mold seemed to develop most readily on summer-milk cheeses wrapped in cloth and stored in moist cellars. Today Blue Cheshire is stored in similar conditions and aerated with skewers to encourage the development of the mold.

A worthy rival of Stilton (though milder), Blue Cheshire is pale orange-gold in color with striking blue veins running through it. It is rich but crumbly-textured and makes an excellent after-dinner cheese paired with a full-bodied red such as Burgundy or a fine Rhône such as Hermitage or Gigondas.

COTSWOLD

ORIGIN	*Gloucester/cow's milk*
TYPE	*semi-firm/48% fat*
TASTE	*Cheddar base with herby, chive flavoring*
APPEARANCE	*rich gold interior flecked with green bits of chive; natural-rind cylinders or blocks*
AVAILABILITY	*general export*

Cotswold is the United States' name for Double Gloucester flavored with chives. Its mellow, rich, Cheddar-like flavor is accented by the fragrant, wild-onion herbiness of chives. It goes very well with dark beer and makes a fine luncheon cheese, served on a good rye bread and with sausages or salad. Light red wines also suit it.

CROWDIE

ORIGIN	*Scotland/cow's milk*
TYPE	*fresh double cream/60% fat*
TASTE	*creamy, buttery*
APPEARANCE	*whitish-yellow creamy paste, white mold rind*
AVAILABILITY	*domestic only*

Also called "cruddy butter," Crowdie is made by combining fresh curd with fresh butter, which gives it its mild, buttery flavor. It is very popular in Scotland as a breakfast food. Refrigerated, it will keep for months.

DERBY

ORIGIN *Derbyshire/cow's milk*
TYPE *semi-firm/45–48% fat*
TASTE *mild*
APPEARANCE *pale orange-gold interior; sold in large cylinders or bricks; natural or paraffin rind*
AVAILABILITY *general export*

A semi-firm Cheddar-style cheese, Derby is flaky in texture but milder in character and generally less interesting than other Cheddars. Those aged up to six months are more pronounced in flavor.

Sage Derby, generously marbled with sage leaves, has a vivid and attractive green color and is much more distinctive than plain Derby. It is a good snack cheese and, due to its herby flavor, is best with beer or ale.

DORSET BLUE

ORIGIN *Dorset, West Country/cow's milk*
TYPE *blue vein/20–40% fat*
TASTE *sharp and salty*
APPEARANCE *chalk-white interior with a single, prominent streak of blue; thin natural rind*
AVAILABILITY *domestic only*

Also known as Blue Vinney, this is a strange and very rare skim-milk cheese. "Vinney" comes from the Old English word "fyniz," meaning "mold." Its very special taste is strong, its smooth texture firm, and sometimes crumbly. Its mold is supposed to have been started in the old days by dipping a horse bridle in the milk! Health regulations did away with that practice and the cheese almost became extinct. Today it is made under modern, controlled conditions but remains rare. Its strong flavors call for robust red wines.

DOUBLE GLOUCESTER

ORIGIN *Gloucester, Somerset, Dorset/cow's milk*
TYPE *semi-firm/45–48% fat*
TASTE *full, mellow, rich*
APPEARANCE *pale to yellow-gold interior; sold in tall cylinders; natural rind*
AVAILABILITY *general export*

Double Gloucester is one of the great English cheeses. It used to be made on farms in small rounds known as "single" Gloucester; nowadays only Double Gloucesters are made. Originally the cheese was made exclusively from the milk of Gloucester cattle, a breed that now has almost died out. Today Gloucester is creamery-made, but its superb keeping qualities and rich, mellow flavors continue to ensure its popularity. It should be savory, never bitter, and the best is satiny and firm in texture.

Gloucester makes a fine luncheon or after-dinner cheese and may be served with beer or a light Bordeaux or Cabernet Sauvignon. The English sometimes wrap it in lettuce leaves or slice it for sandwiches to be served with pickles or jam and honey. It is also good with fresh pears or apples.

DUNLOP

ORIGIN	*Scotland/cow's milk*
TYPE	*semi-firm, Cheddar/45–48% fat*
TASTE	*mild and buttery when young, sharper when aged*
APPEARANCE	*ivory-colored interior; sold in cylinders*
AVAILABILITY	*limited general export*

Moister and milder than Cheddar when it is aged up to two months, Dunlop has a flavor that deepens when it is aged up to four months. Although it grows sharper with age, however, it should remain mellow and is considered too old if bitter. It is especially good with Scottish ale and oatcakes and is also a good toasting cheese.

LANCASHIRE

ORIGIN	*Lancashire/cow's milk*
TYPE	*semi-firm/45% fat*
TASTE	*subtly rich, with lactic tang*
APPEARANCE	*white, close-textured interior; sold in cylinders or blocks*
AVAILABILITY	*limited export*

Softer, moister, and quicker-ripening than Cheddar, Lancashire is the ultimate toasting cheese. At the age of three months, it is as spreadable as butter; aged longer, it becomes firmer and more crumbly in texture. Though mild, it is not bland and develops a richness with more maturity. Farmhouse Lancashire is the best, of course, but is not made in great quantities. It is excellent as a component of cheese sauces or a topping for soup and is considered the premier choice for rarebit.

By itself, Lancashire goes well with fruity red wines or medium-dry sherry.

LEICESTER

ORIGIN	*Leicester/cow's milk*
TYPE	*semi-firm/45–48% fat*
TASTE	*mellow, tangy, with a medium-strong after-taste*
APPEARANCE	*deep orange interior, crumbly texture*
AVAILABILITY	*general export*

The loose, flaky texture of Leicester is higher in moisture content than Cheddar, and the cheese melts in the mouth with a mellow tang. Although Leicester does not have the distinctive character of true Cheddar, it is a fine snack cheese, at its best after ripening for three to nine months, but over-ripe in a year. Its texture makes it difficult to slice without its crumbling, and when poorly stored it develops unpleasantly strong patches of flavor. If the cut edges of the cheese are white, don't buy it, for these are signs of bitterness.

RED CHESHIRE *see* Cheshire

SAGE DERBY *see* Derby

STILTON

ORIGIN	*Leicester, Derbyshire, Nottinghamshire/cow's milk*
TYPE	*blue vein/45% fat*
TASTE	*rich, piquant, with creamy Cheddar under-tones*
APPEARANCE	*white to pale amber interior with evenly spread blue veins; sold in tall cylinders with crusty rind*
AVAILABILITY	*general export*

England's royal blue combines the most distinctive virtues of blue and Cheddar cheeses—the mellow richness of Cheddar is appealingly accented with a moldy tang that is neither overly pungent nor salty. Its copyrighted name dates to the eighteenth century when it was sold to stagecoach passengers in front of the Bell Inn in the small village of Stilton, Huntingdonshire.

Made from rich, whole milk, Stiltons are not pressed, but are turned regularly for at least a week before being removed from stainless steel molds. It is at that time that the brownish crusty rind begins to form. A mild, sourish White Stilton is sold young, before the veins develop, but the blue-veined king is ripened four to six months in cool ripening rooms. The cheese is skewered 300 times or more to encourage the growth of the mold, which develops naturally in the presence

A Homage to Stilton

"Of Stilton it is hard to speak without emotion. Its azure veins avouching noble lineage, it enthrones itself as the world's most regal Blue, exerting, like any true aristocrat, authority without aggressiveness. A Stilton's self-confidence springs from its past (the richest cream and milk) and its future, which can only be one of glory.... There's such divinity doth hedge a Stilton as aureoles no other cheese. It is magisterial."

from an essay by Clifton Fadiman,
"In Praise of Cheese"

of oxygen. In the eighteenth century, a Stilton was not considered ripe until it was crawling with mites. Today the rind is brushed or wiped to keep it clean as the cheese matures.

Stilton is best kept at a cool room-temperature, covered with a cloth. If it dries out, rub it with a cloth soaked in salted water. If you have to refrigerate it, wrap it in a damp cloth. Stilton has a tendency to dry out, but the practice of pouring port wine into the hollowed-out cavity to preserve moisture is *not* recommended and, in fact, detracts from the quality of both the wine and the cheese. A whole Stilton keeps best if cut horizontally and then sliced into wedge-shaped portions for serving.

Stilton stands by itself, accompanied only by a glass of port or full-bodied Burgundy and perhaps a biscuit or dried fruit.

WENSLEYDALE

ORIGIN	*Yorkshire/cow's milk*
TYPE	*semi-firm, blue vein/45% fat*
TASTE	*White is fresh and buttermilk-like, richer with age; Blue is rich with a creamy tang and fine aftertaste*
APPEARANCE	*white or blue-veined interior; sold in cylinders or blocks*
AVAILABILITY	*general export*

White Wensleydale, made from a finely cut curd that is lightly pressed, has a high moisture content. Ripened only up to three weeks, it should be eaten when it is young and fresh. Its tangy flavor and chalky, smooth texture are superb with fresh apples, pears, and green grapes; it is the cheese *par excellence* with apple pie. When more mature its flavor becomes richer and faintly sweet, and it develops a very attractive aftertaste. Dry, fruity white wines make excellent companions to White Wensleydale.

Blue Wensleydale is considered a great delicacy. It is much more robust in flavor and needs at least six months to mature. Its smooth texture is creamier than Stilton and its flavor a bit milder. Many people prefer it for that reason, although it is harder to come by. Dry reds are its best accompaniment.

WINDSOR RED

A variation of Cheddar, flavored with a red berry juice that gives its pale yellow interior a pink-marbled effect.

♦♦♦

FRANCE

o one takes cheese more seriously—or treats it more lovingly—than the French, whether they are making it, buying it, serving it, or eating it. It is a staple of the everyday table. It can also be the *crescendo* of a great meal, a showcase for the principal wine of the evening. Annual per capita consumption is the largest in the world: On the average, nearly 38 pounds of cheese are consumed by each person every year.

The number and variety of French cheeses are astonishing. France produces some 400 cheeses. Most are produced from cow's milk, but there are numerous sheep's and goat's milk cheeses as well. Two of France's most famous cheeses—Brie and Roquefort—vie for the world title of *le roi des fromages.* So far, throughout their very long history the contest is a stand-off that awards the title to both!

Not only does France have cheeses that are individually famous; she has whole *groups* of cheeses that are eagerly sought after: the lush, rich double and triple creams like Brillat-Savarin, L'Explorateur, Boursault; the delectable soft-ripened Brie, Camembert, Coulommiers; the fragrant mountain cheeses like Beaufort, Gruyère, Tomme de Pyrénées; the tangy, piquant *chèvres,* or goat cheeses; the pungent and odiferous Livarot, Maroilles, Pont L'Evêque; the slightly milder monastery cheeses such as Munster or Port Salut; and, of course, *les bleus:* Roquefort, Bleu de Bresse, Pipo Crem', Fourme d'Ambert, and a number of others.

Cheeses are produced in every corner of France, with heaviest concentrations in the Auvergne (home of several blues and Cantal), the Loire Valley and Poitou *(chèvres),* the mountains of the Jura, the Vosges in Alsace and the Pyrénées, and the Ile de France surrounding Paris.

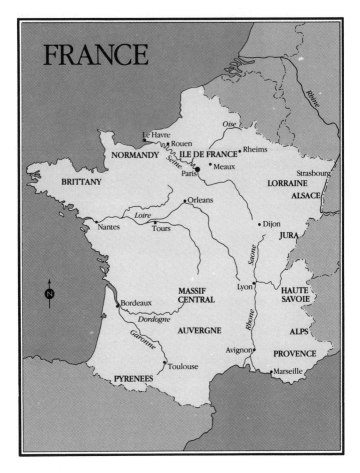

France's dairyland, however, is Normandy. Just as a wine road (Route des Grands Vins) winds through Burgundy, a "cheese road" wends its way through Normandy, connecting the towns that have fostered some of the country's most distinctive cheeses: Camembert, Livarot and Pont L'Evêque. Here, greener pastures give some of the richest cow's milk. Farm-made Camembert, produced from raw milk *(lait crû)* and ripened on straw mats, is a treasure Parisians constantly search out, but it is increasingly hard to come by.

Tourist travel to France has created a worldwide demand for French cheeses that has had a significant impact on cheese production in the last decade or so. It has spawned a factory industry that can better fulfill demand, though not without some sacrifice of quality and, in some cases, of the highly individual character for which certain cheeses are famous. The blandness of many factory-made Brie and Camembert are two examples. Genuinely original versions of each are now relatively rare. In addition, many new cheeses have been developed to satisfy the increasing clamor for popular types. Yet the demand for the French classics is unceasing and a whole cadre of specialty cheese shops has sprung up to bring them to us. Getting to know French cheeses is an adventure that demands something of you, rather like getting to know French wines.

In both cases, it's worth the effort.

Cheese Guide

BANON

ORIGIN	*Provence/usually goat's milk*
TYPE	*chèvre/45% fat*
TASTE TASTE	*mild and lactic to savory*
APPEARANCE	*4- to 7-ounce discs wrapped in green leaves and tied with rafia; white, creamy or chalky interior; natural rind*
AVAILABILITY	*general export*

This natural-rind cheese is usually made from goat's milk, but sometimes from sheep's or cow's milk or a mixture of the two. Banon is cured in leaves and sometimes washed in *marc* over a period of two to eight weeks. It is most commonly either mild and lactic, or milky; as it ages it loses moisture and becomes more piquant. Leaves should not be dark, dried out, or mottled with mold when the cheese is purchased, and the cheese itself should be fairly firm. A hard texture is a sign that it is drying out.

Banon is a good summer luncheon cheese that goes well with dry, fruity whites such as Sancerre or Pouilly-Fumé, Tavel rosé, or light, fruity red wines.

BEAUFORT (also Gruyère de Beaufort)

ORIGIN	*Savoie/cow's milk*
TYPE	*semi-firm, Swiss/50% fat*
TASTE	*mellow, smooth, sometimes stronger*
APPEARANCE	*wheels up to 125 pounds with natural rough rinds; pale yellow interior with few holes*
AVAILABILITY	*general export*

Similar to Swiss GRUYÈRE this cheese is made in the alpine regions of the Jura and Savoie of eastern France. It is mild and supple with Swiss-like flavors but very few small holes. *Beaufort haut-montagne*, which is made from the milk of cows that summer high in the alpine pastures and aged six months or longer, is richer in character and more flavorful. Avoid cheeses with cracked rind, too many holes, rubbery texture, or excessive saltiness.

Beaufort is fine as a snack cheese with fresh fruit and dry but fruity white or red wines.

BEAUMONT

ORIGIN	*Haut-Savoie/cow's milk*
TYPE	*semi-soft/50% fat*
TASTE	*savory, full-flavored*
APPEARANCE	*large discs with light ochre, firm rinds; yellow smooth interior*
AVAILABILITY	*general export*

A supple-textured cheese similar to such monastery cheeses as Saint-Paulin, Beaumont is somewhat more vividly flavored and becomes earthier in flavor and darker in color as it matures. It will keep for a few weeks if well-wrapped and refrigerated. Avoid improperly cured ones with unnaturally bulging or cracked rinds.

Beaumont is enjoyed in France with wines of the Savoy such as Crèpy or Seyssel; Pinot Blanc is also a good choice, as are reds from the Côtes du Rhône.

BELLE BRESSANE

ORIGIN	*Bresse/cow's milk*
TYPE	*blue vein/50% fat*
TASTE	*mild and creamy, somewhat piquant but not sharp*
APPEARANCE	*cake-like cylinders with hole in center; whitish rind flecked with orange; ivory interior with blue veins*
AVAILABILITY	*general export*

This is one of the milder blues from Grièges, a town in the alpine region of Bresse. The extra bit of richness makes it creamy and somewhat similar to PIPO CREM'. A good choice when you want a less piquant blue, and it goes well with sturdy red wines from Burgundy or the Rhône. Lightly sweet whites will also suit this cheese.

BLEU

The French term for blue-veined cheeses injected with spores of *Penicillium glaucum*. Most French blues are made from cow's milk, except for Roquefort, which is made from sheep's milk. Generally, the region in which the cheese is produced is part of the name, as in BLEU DE BRESSE or BLEU D'AUVERGNE. Blues are often referred to as *persillé*, or parsleyed, because the network of blue-green veins resembles sprigs of parsley. The flavors range from creamy to very intense and piquant, and they require sturdy red wines.

BLEU D'AUVERGNE

ORIGIN *Auvergne/cow's milk*
TYPE *blue vein/45% fat*
TASTE *salty, creamy, piquant*
APPEARANCE *whitish yellow interior with well-developed blue mold; thin rind; sold in foil-wrapped, 4-inch-tall cylinders*
AVAILABILITY *general export*

This is one of the best and most intensely flavored French blues. When it is properly aged, the texture is creamy rather than crumbly, the flavors not overly strong or sharp. It originated in the nineteenth century as an imitation of Roquefort, with the distinction that it uses cow's milk instead of sheep's milk. Some Bleu d'Auvergne is still made on mountain farms; those that are particularly good carry the name of *Thiezac*. They are strong and densely blue but can be mellowed by mixing with sweet butter. Those from Laqueuille are milder. They are best with full-bodied Rhône reds such as Hermitage or *Gigondas*.

BLEU DE BRESSE

ORIGIN *Eastern France/cow's milk*
TYPE *blue vein/50% fat*
TASTE *creamy, milder than most blues*
APPEARANCE *small cylinders with whitish rinds; whitish interior with blue streaks or splotches; sometimes boxed or wrapped*
AVAILABILITY *general export*

A creamy, moist French blue with mild but savory flavors and a soft, spreadable texture, Bleu de Bresse is similar to Gorgonzola and Pipo Crem'. Exported cheeses are occasionally overripe with crumbly textures, heavy mold, and ammoniated flavors. Even these, however, have their fans among lovers of *bleu*. Bleu de Bresse is one of the most popular blues, especially prized in early spring in France when its consistency is very soft and creamy.

It is best with unflavored crackers, ripe pears, and rich wines such as Saint-Emilion or Sonoma County Cabernets.

BLEU DES CAUSSES

ORIGIN *Auvergne/cow's milk*
TYPE *blue vein/45% fat*
TASTE *full, savory flavors*
APPEARANCE *ivory interior with lacy blue veins; sold in rindless foil-wrapped cylinders*
AVAILABILITY *limited export*

A fine blue similar to Bleu d'Auvergne, though not quite as intense. Bleu des Causses should not be sharp, too strong in aroma, or dry and crumbly. Still, it is one of the more assertive cow's milk blues, made near the Roquefort region and aged in caves or humid cellars for two to three months.

Used in salads, as a snack, or as an after-dinner cheese, Bleu des Causses calls for robust reds such as Châteauneuf du Pape, Côte Rotie, or California Syrah.

BLEU DE CORSE

A sheep's milk blue made on the highland plateaus of Corsica, Bleu de Corse is modeled after ROQUEFORT. Cured in caves, it is pungent and rich though sometimes only lightly veined. It is rarely exported.

BLEU DU HAUT-JURA (also Bleu de Gex or Bleu de Septmoncel)

ORIGIN	*Jura/cow's milk*
TYPE	*blue vein/45% fat*
TASTE	*tangy, savory, milder than most blues*
APPEARANCE	*sold in thick wheels with grayish rinds; ivory interior with blue streaks*
AVAILABILITY	*limited export*

Bleu du Haut-Jura is the generic name for blues from Gex, Septmoncel and elsewhere in the region. *Bleu de Gex* is more commonly seen outside France. Slightly milder in flavor than most blue veins, it is said to be "the blue for people who don't like blues." This is true enough when the veining is light, but in its more mature versions it can be quite savory and faintly bitter. An appealing blue, it is good with Beaujolais, particularly one of the *crus* such as Fleurie or Saint-Amour, or with other fruity reds.

Bleu de Septmoncel is very similar to Gex; both cheeses are produced in the Jura mountains but in different areas.

BONBEL

Brand name of exported, bland, semi-soft SAINT PAULIN.

BONDON

Small cylinders of NEUFCHÂTEL.

BOUILLE, LA

A small cylindrical double cream similar to MONSIEUR FROMAGE of Normandy, La Bouille has a white bloomy rind flecked with orange and a soft, creamy, savory paste.

BOURSAULT

ORIGIN	*northern France/cow's milk*
TYPE	*triple cream/75% fat*
TASTE	*rich, creamy, savory*
APPEARANCE	*small, paper-wrapped cylinders; soft, creamy interior with bloomy rind*
AVAILABILITY	*general export*

One of the most popular of the triple creams, Boursault is

enriched with fresh cream. As a soft-ripened cheese it ripens inside its snowy rind to a luscious, salty paste with a consistency almost like whipped cream. Avoid those with discolored paper wrapping or sagging shape.

BOURSIN

ORIGIN	*Normandy, Ile de France/cow's milk*
TYPE	*triple cream/70–75% fat*
TASTE	*rich, savory, often herb-flavored*
APPEARANCE	*small foil-wrapped cylinders; rindless; white creamy paste, flecked with seasonings*
AVAILABILITY	*general export*

Boursin is a triple cream, especially popular in versions flavored with garlic, herbs, or cracked pepper. It has a smooth, buttery texture and rich, creamy flavors often piquant with seasonings. It is good with dry white wines from the Loire Valley or Macon, as well as with fruity reds. In addition, Boursin is delicious as a breakfast cheese with bagels and black coffee.

BREBIGNOL

A semi-firm sheep's cheese made in the Pyrénées region of southwestern France, Brebignol has the subtle but savory tang that characterizes many sheep's milk cheeses. It is mainly a snack or lunch cheese, best accompanied by fruity wines. Not widely exported.

BREBIS FRAIS DU ROUERGUE

ORIGIN	*Auvergne/ewe's milk*
TYPE	*sheep, fresh/45% fat*
TASTE	*fresh, rich, mild*
APPEARANCE	*chalky white, smooth interior; sold in containers*
AVAILABILITY	*limited export*

Brebis Frais du Rouergue is a fresh sheep's milk cheese from the Roquefort region. Though quite rich, it has a delicate—and delicious—milky tang. A fine breakfast or luncheon cheese, Brebis Frais is good with fresh or preserved fruit, light wines, or black coffee.

BRIE (also Brie de Meaux, Brie de Melun, or Coulommiers)

ORIGIN	*Ile de France/cow's milk*
TYPE	*soft-ripened/45% fat*
TASTE	*creamy, savory with a fruity tang and rich aftertaste*
APPEARANCE	*round, flat discs of 2 or 4 pounds with white rinds flecked with gold or russet pigments; high-gloss, cream-colored paste*
AVAILABILITY	*general export*

Specialty cheese shops claim to sell more Brie than any other cheese, so popular has this import become. There are Bries and there are Bries, however. The original, *Brie de Meaux,* was known at least as far back as the eighth century. One reference indicates that Charlemagne knew it, and in 1815, when the French diplomat Talleyrand introduced it at the Congress of Vienna, it was proclaimed by all present as the "king of cheeses."

Brie made from unpasteurized milk and produced on farmsteads around Meaux or Melun (famous cheese towns a few miles outside of Paris) counts, at peak ripeness, among the most sublime of taste experiences. The flavor was once described as "part mushroom, part cream, part cognac, part earth...with a shade of truffle...and something of the scent of ripe Anjou pears." Unpasteurized Bries are generally only available in Europe, and cannot be legally imported to the United States.

Most exported Bries are made from pasteurized milk by factories whose quality varies. At perfect ripeness they are still among the most delectable of cheeses. But a lot of them are bland or underripe. Learning to select a fine Brie takes practice and attention, and good ones may have to be searched out. When underripe, Brie has a hard, chalky core at the center. Such a cheese will never ripen fully. Look instead for an even, creamy color and a smooth paste that is plump inside its rind. When not fully ripe, a whole Brie will feel somewhat firm. If you buy Brie in this condition, store it in a cool place or in the warmest part of the refrigerator for a couple of days. Remove it to room temperature two hours before serving. A fully ripe Brie is somewhat yielding to the touch, perhaps even bulging a bit inside the rind, which will have begun to develop brownish edges and show coloration across the rind. Brie has a brief life, so if it has not softened and matured in a few days, you can be reasonably sure that it probably won't soften and mature at all. It will simply dry out and harden, the paste inside will darken, and the smell will become more ammoniated.

On the other hand, the best Brie will not be overly runny either. The French say that a good Brie should ooze, not run. Once cut, it does not ripen further, which is why it is critical to buy it at just the right moment and to serve it as soon as possible. One cannot buy much in advance. It is very perishable, especially when perfectly ripe, and therefore it is best to buy only the exact amount you are sure you will need for the occasion.

The bloomy rinds of Brie de Meaux and Brie de Melun, both of which come in thin, flat, pancake-like discs over a foot in diameter, show a reddish pigment dusted in the rind and sometimes the faint impression of the straw mats on which they were ripened. This is a good sign, especially if the cheese is plump and resilient to the touch. But if the rind is dry and tough, or gummy and sagging, or smells strongly of ammonia, it may be overripe—here your own taste preference must be your guide. Some people like them that way. The rind is edible, but don't hesitate to trim it off if you prefer. In France it is eaten both ways.

Rarest of the Bries is Brie de Meaux *fermier*—farm-produced, inimitably gorgeous, with the texture of rich honey. It is not widely available, even in France. Made solely of *lait crû* (raw milk), it has a subtle but penetrating and lingering savor that one must taste if one is to comprehend the difference between it and the mild, pleasant Bries we are mostly accustomed to.

Brie de Melun is a little deeper in color, slightly earthier in character and slightly less complex than Brie de Meaux, though some will argue it the other way round. Coulommiers is made in thicker rounds of smaller diameter than most Bries. It is milder than those from Meaux or Melun and more like Camembert.

Bries are classic after-dinner cheeses with red or white wines. Whole wheels make a dashing display for wine tastings or cocktail parties.

BRILLAT-SAVARIN

ORIGIN	*France/cow's milk*
TYPE	*triple cream/75% fat*
TASTE	*creamy, luscious, faintly sour*
APPEARANCE	*white, bloomy-rind discs of creamy white paste*
AVAILABILITY	*general export*

A popular brand of triple cream, Brillat-Savarin is excellent as a dessert with Meedjol dates and German Spätlese or Auslese, or with Champagne biscuits and Champagne.

BRIN D'AMOUR (also Fleur du Maquis)

ORIGIN	*Corsica/goat's or sheep's milk*
TYPE	*semi-firm/45% fat*
TASTE	*subtle but savory, herby*
APPEARANCE	*blocks with thin, natural rinds; chalk-white, smooth interior*
AVAILABILITY	*limited export*

This delectable (and expensive) "morsel of love" comes from the central plateau of Corsica where sheep and goats graze on wild thyme, rosemary, coriander, and other herbs. Most are made from sheep's milk, but some are made from a mixture of goat's and sheep's milk. Brin d'Amour is cured for three months with the same aromatic herbs that the animals feed upon and is shipped with the herbs clinging to the rind.

The delicate herby flavors and sheepy tang of this cheese are excellent with full-bodied white Burgundies or reds from the Rhône.

BÛCHE LORRAINE

A small, loaf-shaped DOUBLE CREAM with a downy white rind and mild Brie-like flavors.

BÛCHERON

ORIGIN	*Poitou/goat's milk*
TYPE	*chèvre, soft/45% fat*
TASTE	*mild, savory tang*
APPEARANCE	*5-pound logs with white rinds, occasionally covered with black ash*
AVAILABILITY	*general export*

A popular, soft, chalky CHÈVRE, Bûcheron is tangy but mild, rich, and sometimes quite spreadable. It should not be yellowed or dried out. It goes well with crisp, dry whites or light red wines.

CABECOU see Chabichou

CALVADOUX

ORIGIN	*Normandy/cow's milk*
TYPE	*soft-ripened/45% fat*
TASTE	*assertive, with a raunchy tang*
APPEARANCE	*flat cylinder with orange-gold rind, ochre paste*
AVAILABILITY	*general export*

A fairly new variety of surface-ripened cheese, Calvadoux is also similar to other monastery types such as PONT L'EVÊQUE, after which it is modeled. The name comes from the fact that it is produced in Calvados country. When very ripe, it oozes thickly and takes on pungent flavors and aromas.

CAMEMBERT

ORIGIN	*Normandy/cow's milk*
TYPE	*soft-ripened/45% fat*
TASTE	*creamy, Brie-like but milder*
APPEARANCE	*small discs; white downy rind with goldish-orange flecks; pale, creamy paste*
AVAILABILITY	*general export*

A classic among world cheeses, Camembert is widely imitated in many countries. Fine Camembert, however, is exceedingly hard to come by. Just as Americans search for the perfect Brie, the French go after Camembert *à point*. It is a great coup at Paris parties to serve a farm-made variety that is at ripe perfection—a state that doesn't last beyond a day and a half at most. Like Brie, it should ooze thickly and creamily, or "exude," as one gastronome put it. But it is better to have faintly underripe than overripe Camembert, as it tends to become bitter and ammoniated to the point of rankness when overly ripe.

This cheese is said to have been invented by a farmer's wife named Marie Harel, to whom a statue was erected in her home town of Vimoutiers in Normandy. Camembert was christened by Napoleon. Stopping for lunch in the little town of Camembert near Vimoutiers, he is said to have leaped to his feet and kissed the serving maid who brought him the cheese.

Most Camembert today is factory-made and therefore fairly uniform in quality, but those made by small dairies or on farms can still be highly individual cheeses that vary subtly from season to season (look for *Le Rustique, La Normandie*). When perfectly ripe, Camembert will have a pronounced aroma, pleasantly piquant and redolent of its special mold *Penicillium camemberti,* and rich creamy flavors that end on a distinctive tangy note. Quite extraordinary. Supermarket versions are likely to be bland or bitter, especially those in cans.

It is best to buy the whole cheese since it is small, usually boxed in cardboard or chipwood. Like Brie, it should be plump and full inside its rind and soft to the touch. Those that have shrunk away from the box or have hardened rind edges may be overripe.

In Normandy, Camembert is usually accompanied by cider, since apples are as ubiquitous there as dairy cows. It is also fine with Bordeaux reds or California Cabernets and Merlots.

CAMPAGNOLE

Developed rather recently, this goat's milk blue is made with *roqueforti* mold. It is tart, fresh, and chalk white, with a blue vein running through the center. It is not widely exported.

CANTAL (also Fourme de Cantal)

ORIGIN	*Auvergne/cow's milk*
TYPE	*semi-firm/45% fat*
TASTE	*mellow, nutty, smooth*
APPEARANCE	*large cylinders with greyish-beige rinds; smooth yellow interior*
AVAILABILITY	*limited export*

This cheese is produced only in the department of Cantal in central France, its name protected under the laws of *appellation controlée.* One of France's oldest cheeses, it is somewhat like Cheddar in flavor. The texture of young cheeses aged three to six months is smooth and supple, rather like an American Colby Cheddar. Its mellow, nutty flavor begins to sharpen and deepen after that, and the texture becomes firmer and more crumbly. Its wholesome, milky flavors make Cantal an excellent snack cheese, but well-aged versions are superb with solid red wines after dinner, or with beer.

CAPRICE DES DIEUX

ORIGIN	*Haut-Marne/cow's milk*
TYPE	*double cream/60% fat*
TASTE	*rich, mild, creamy*

APPEARANCE	*flat, oval discs with downy white rind and pale, soft interior*
AVAILABILITY	*general export*

One of the best known double creams, Caprice des Dieux is similar to Brie and Camembert, but is enriched with cream. When ripe, the paste should be resiliently soft; the rind tinged with light orange. Overripe cheeses have hardened rinds, distorted shapes, and the smell of ammonia. Caprice des Dieux is good with Bordeaux reds, wafers, and grapes.

CAPRICETTE

Capricette is a creamy, fresh goat cheese (CHÈVRE) that comes in small, frosty white cakes that have mild flavors and a spreadable texture.

CAPRICORNE

Made in the shape of a flat wheel, this *chèvre* has a downy white rind and a hole in its center. Inside the thin rind, the cheese has a dryish texture (it may be creamy near the rind) and sharp, salty flavors. It is very appealing with crisp white wines such as Sancerre or Chablis.

CARRÉ DE L'EST

ORIGIN	*northeastern France/cow's milk*
TYPE	*soft-ripened/45–50% fat*
TASTE	*mild, creamy, mushroomy*
APPEARANCE	*small squares with downy rinds and soft, ivory paste*
AVAILABILITY	*general export*

A French classic of the minor leagues, Carré de l'Est is made in Lorraine and the Champagne region. The name means "square of the East." It is similar to Camembert in flavor and texture but develops a light mushroom aroma when ripe. It makes an enjoyable snack or after-dinner cheese served with firm-textured dark breads and fruity red wines.

CHABICHOU (also Cabécou)

ORIGIN	*Poitou/goat's milk*
TYPE	*chèvre, soft/45% fat*
TASTE	*assertive goaty tang*
APPEARANCE	*sold in small cones with bluish-grey rind, or small white logs with white rind; soft, chalk-white interior*
AVAILABILITY	*limited export*

Chabichou (the name means "little goat") is a very tasty *chèvre* from the Loire Valley with a zesty tang that sharpens with age. Farm-produced Chabis have bluish rinds flecked with reddish-brown. Like all soft cheeses, it is considered overripe if it appears dark and shrunken. Chabichou is good with full-bodied reds such as Juliénas or Paso Robles.

CHAMOIS D'OR

Almost a double crème (52% fat), this soft-ripened cheese has a bloomy rind. As a cross between Brie and Camembert it doesn't quite come off. It is modeled after Brie de Coulommiers but is rather lacking in interesting character. Creamy enough, it is a somewhat bland but agreeable addition to the cheese board and goes with a variety of red or white wines.

CHAOURCE

ORIGIN	*Champagne/cow's milk*
TYPE	*soft-ripened/45%–50% fat*
TASTE	*rich, very creamy, fruity*
APPEARANCE	*flat cylinders 5 inches in diameter with bloomy white rinds; ivory center*
AVAILABILITY	*general export*

Chaource, named for a leading market town in the Champagne region, is very similar to Camembert or Coulommiers. Although it lacks the complexity of either, it is lusciously rich and creamy, and gets stronger and saltier as it matures, ultimately developing a pronounced mushroom aroma and an acidic edge. A popular choice for the after-dinner cheese tray, it goes well with light Burgundies; it is also good with Mâcon Blanc, Chardonnay, or other full-bodied white wines.

CHAUMES

ORIGIN	*France/cow's milk*
TYPE	*monastery/45% fat*
TASTE	*assertive, tangy*
APPEARANCE	*large, flat orange disc, soft yellow center*
AVAILABILITY	*general export*

A soft-ripened cheese with a semi-soft texture and an assertive aroma like Munster, Chaumes comes in a flat, round, pancake-style disc with a deep orange, washed-rind surface. Numerous small holes dot the pale yellow paste. Its pronounced flavors have a richness and a faint edge of bitterness that turns to stinkiness when the cheese is very ripe. Chaumes needs a Pilsner-style lager beer or a very full-bodied red to stand up to it.

CHÈVRES

Fromage de chèvre, or goat cheese, accounts for less than three percent of the total cheese production in France, yet it is one of the most popular types. A great many come from farms or cooperatives along the Loire River and Poitou to the south, but they are also produced in other regions. Cheese labeled *pur chèvre* is supposed to be all goat's milk, others may include some cow's milk, but all exhibit the fresh, tart zing common to goat cheese. They range in texture from soft, moist, and creamy to somewhat dry and sliceable, and

---

Cheese and Herbs

One of the most appetizing ways to serve a fresh *chèvre* is gently bathed in fine olive oil and sprinkled with thyme. Use only fresh rindless cylinders of *chèvres* and just enough French or Italian olive oil to coat the cheese lightly, then sprinkle the herbs on top.

The herbiness of thyme provides the perfect accent for the dry tang of young *chèvres*, but Herbes de Provences may also be used. Do not refrigerate as the oil will solidify and discolor. Serve with crusty French bread.

Pont l'Evêque, Chaumes, Rollot, Vieux Pané, or other washed-rind cheeses are similarly herb-enhanced by sprinkling fennel or anise seed on the rind. Let stand a day or overnight to absorb the flavor and brush away the herbs before cutting and serving.

---

they are always chalk white. They are molded into numerous shapes: cones, pyramids, logs, cylinders, small discs. Some have bloomy white rinds, others are *cendré* (coated in edible vegetable ash that preserves moisture), still others are wrapped in leaves or sprinkled with pepper or herbs. Specialty cheese shops carry as many as 20 or 30 different *chèvres.* They will keep a couple of weeks if refrigerated, but after three weeks or so they become dried out and ammoniated. They are always tart and tangy to some degree but should not be overly acidic or biting, or too sour.

There are too many varieties to include in this volume but some of the better-known ones have their own entries: Banon, Lezay, Sainte-Maure, Géant, Bûcheron, Montrachet, Chevrette, Saint-Marcellin. Goat cheeses, with their mild or bracing zest, are excellent with dry, crisp white wines like Sancerre, Mâcon, Chablis, or with reds like Chinon, Santenay, Pinot Noir, or Beaujolais.

CHEVROTIN

One of the milder CHÈVRE, or goat cheese, that comes in cones or small cylinders.

CHIBERTA see Tourton

CLOCHETTE CHAPUT

This small CHÈVRES is produced in the shape of a bell (*clochette* means "little bell"). It has a fleecy rind and a goaty, piquant tang. Best when very fresh and served with crisp, dry white wines.

COEUR DE BRAY

A soft, creamy cheese similar to NEUFCHATEL, Coeur de Bray has a bloomy white rind and is shaped like a heart. It comes from the Pays de Bray in upper Normandy.

COMTÉ (also Gruyère de Comté or French Gruyère)

ORIGIN	*Franche Comté, Savoie/cow's milk*
TYPE	*semi-firm, Swiss/45% fat*
TASTE	*mellow, fruity, nutty*
APPEARANCE	*large cylinders with gold rind; pale ochre paste with scattered hazelnut-sized holes*
AVAILABILITY	*limited export*

This cousin to BEAUFORT and EMMENTAL is part of the family of French GRUYÈRES. It has typically nutty, Swiss-like flavors but is a little more vivid and less sweet. Comté is widely used in cooking, for fondues as well as in omelets, quiche, and the French grilled sandwich known as *croque-monsieur.*

As a snack, lunch, or after-dinner cheese, Comté is well-suited to fruity wines, whether white, red, or rosé, and to beer.

COROLLE DU POITOU

ORIGIN	*Poitou/cow's milk*
TYPE	*double cream/60% fat*
TASTE	*rich, creamy, tangy finish*
APPEARANCE	*wheels with center hole, white bloomy rind; chalky center surrounded by creamy, ivory paste*
AVAILABILITY	*general export*

This part of France (Poitou) is noted mostly for its goat cheeses, but the soft-ripened Corolle (named for its shape, which resembles a crown) is a new, cow's milk cheese, developed to capitalize on the popularity of Brie and double creams. Very rich and mild, it slices like angel-food cake—indeed, some would consider it angel's food.

COULOMMIERS (also Brie de Coulommiers)

ORIGIN	*Ile de France/cow's milk*
TYPE	*soft-ripened/45–50% fat*
TASTE	*creamy, Brie-like*
APPEARANCE	*flat cylinders 5 inches in diameter; white bloomy rind; creamy ivory interior*
AVAILABILITY	*limited export*

From the town of Coulommiers near Meaux, this cheese is kissing cousin to BRIE DE MEAUX, although it is less fragile and not quite as distinctive in flavor. Often confused with small Brie, it is in fact thicker and tends to keep better, developing a nutty tang when ripe. It is a good bet for dinner parties where a large Brie would be too big. One of the best brands is *Le Fougerou,* whose rind is ornamented by a fern leaf. It should be soft and yielding to the touch; if not, it may show a hard, chalky core when cut. Avoid ammoniated, overripe cheeses with hard or smelly rinds.

This cheese is good with crisp French bread and most red wines.

CROTTIN DE CHAVIGNOL

ORIGIN	*Berry/goat's milk*
TYPE	*chèvre/45% fat*
TASTE	*dry and piquant to quite sharp*
APPEARANCE	*small, flat-bottomed balls; white rind splotched with brown; chalky interior*
AVAILABILITY	*limited export*

Local farmers named this little cheese (*crottin* means "horse droppings") for its shape and the darkened color of well-aged versions. When young and fresh—as it often is in the town of Sancerre—it is deliciously goaty and tangy, delightful when spread on French bread and washed down with the local white wines, Sancerre or Pouilly-Fumé.

With age, however, it becomes quite sharp and strong and develops a dry, tough rind. Exported versions generally fall somewhere in between.

CROTTIN POIVRE

ORIGIN	*Pyrénées, Auvergne/cow's or ewe's milk*
TYPE	*semi-firm/45% fat*
TASTE	*savory, mildly salty, peppery*
APPEARANCE	*stocky cylinders with grooved black rinds; pale gold interior flecked with cracked pepper*
AVAILABILITY	*limited export*

A rustic, savory close-textured cheese studded with pepper-corns, it has a zesty character and is sometimes hard enough for grating.

CURÉ NANTAIS (also Fromage du Curé)

ORIGIN	*Brittany/cow's milk*
TYPE	*monastery, soft/40% fat*
TASTE	*assertive flavor and aroma*
APPEARANCE	*small, rounded squares with orange-gold rind; soft yellow interior*
AVAILABILITY	*limited export*

A washed rind-cheese, Curé Nantais becomes quite pungent in flavor and aroma as it ages, falling somewhere between Saint-Paulin and Pont l'Evêque. Developed by a parish priest near Nantes, it is also known as *Fromage du Curé*. Seldom exported, it is delicious with local wines such as Muscadet or Gros Plant du Pays.

DOLMEN

This CHÈVRE comes in the shape of trapezoidal bricks from Poitou. It is rich, tangy, not overly sharp, and is sometimes ash-coated.

DOUX DE MONTAGNE (also Pain de Pyrénées)

ORIGIN	*Pyrénées/cow's milk*
TYPE	*semi-firm/45% fat*
TASTE	*mellow, sweet, fruity*
APPEARANCE	*sold in cylinders; pale yellow interior with irregular holes; dark rind*
AVAILABILITY	*general export*

Doux de Montagne is a relatively recently developed cheese from the foothill region of the Pyrénées in southwestern France. Its name means "sweet of the mountain" and fairly describes its mellow nuttiness. Aged versions have a more interesting character, but exports for the most part are young, semi-soft, and have waxed rinds.

Country reds, such as Corbières, Fitou, Cahors, or regional Bordeaux, go well with it.

EMMENTAL

ORIGIN	*Franche Comté, Savoie/cow's milk*
TYPE	*semi-firm/45% fat*
TASTE	*mild, nutty*
APPEARANCE	*sold in large wheels with convex sides; gold rind; pale yellow interior with many large holes*
AVAILABILITY	*general export*

The French version of Switzerland Swiss may have been made in the eastern mountains as early as the sixteenth century. Like the other French Gruyères, BEAUFORT and COMTÉ, it has mellow, nutty flavors and is widely used for snacks and cooking, as it grates well and melts easily.

Fruity red or white wines suit it well, as does cider or beer.

EPOISSES

ORIGIN	*Burgundy/cow's milk*
TYPE	*monastery, soft/45% fat*
TASTE	*mild with tangy finish to quite strong*
APPEARANCE	*small, thick cylinders; light orange to reddish rind; creamy-soft ivory paste*
AVAILABILITY	*limited export*

One of the classic washed-rind cheeses, Epoisses is traditionally cured in salt water and *marc de Bourgogne* (*eau-de-vie* from grape pomace). It has a fine character, tangy and faintly acid when young, becoming very pronounced in flavor and aroma with age, like Pont L'Evêque. The rind is sometimes dusted with fennel or pepper. A cheeselover's cheese, Epoisses is best with full-bodied red Burgundies from the Côte de Nuits.

EWE ROUERGUE

A lightly-veined blue cheese made from ewe's milk in the south of France. Like most sheep cheese, it is tangy and assertive but not widely exported.

EXCELSIOR

ORIGIN	*Normandy/cow's milk*
TYPE	*triple cream/72% fat*
TASTE	*mild, creamy, faintly nutty*
APPEARANCE	*small, fat cylinders with snowy rinds, soft ivory interior*
AVAILABILITY	*general export*

Excelsior, enriched with cream, was invented nearly a hundred years ago in a Norman dairy. Now factory-made, it is one of the most popular triple creams, only slightly less rich than EXPLORATEUR, but with a little more complexity of character. Serve with red Burgundy, Champagne or other sparkling wines.

EXPLORATEUR

ORIGIN	*Ile de France/cow's milk*
TYPE	*triple cream/75% fat*
TASTE	*unctuously rich, creamy*
APPEARANCE	*small, thick cylinders with white rinds, soft ivory paste*
AVAILABILITY	*general export*

Although this cheese is sometimes described as a triple-cream Brie, its rich creaminess masks the character that might be present in a cheese of lower fat content. Extravagantly rich and creamy, Explorateur has a faintly piquant finish when perfectly ripe. When too old, its ammoniated rind destroys its delicate flavors. It is best with fruity, dry white wines or light reds.

FEUILLES DE DREUX

ORIGIN	*Ile de France/cow's milk*
TYPE	*soft-ripened/40–45% fat*
TASTE	*creamy, Brie-like but fruitier*
APPEARANCE	*flat discs of 6 inches in diameter wrapped in brown chestnut leaves; soft, creamy, yellow interior*
AVAILABILITY	*general export*

Feuilles de Dreux is a fast-ripening, quickly perishable cheese made on farms or in small factories north of Chartres in the town of Dreux, sometimes from partially skimmed milk. It is an excellent alternative to Brie de Meaux or farm-produced Camembert. Watch out for an intense ammonia smell and dried out or rotted leaves, which indicates, of course, that the cheese is too old.

FOL AMOUR

A brand of soft-ripened double cream produced in northern France. General export.

FONTAINEBLEAU

A fresh cheese enriched with whipped cream, Fontainebleau is normally eaten with berries or preserved fruit. It should be as fresh as possible.

FONTAL

French Fontina.

LE FOUGEROU *see* Coulommiers

FOURME D'AMBERT

ORIGIN	*Auvergne/cow's milk*
TYPE	*blue-vein/45% fat*
TASTE	*assertive blue, faintly bitter*
APPEARANCE	*comes in tall slender cylinders; dense veining; whitish interior*
AVAILABILITY	*limited export*

This is one of the more intense French *bleus,* distinguished by a salty, slightly bitter bite that appeals to many blue cheese *aficionados.* The texture is rich and softly crumbly and should not be dried out. It is similar to BLEU D'AUVERGNE but stronger and demands sturdy reds such as Châteauneuf-du-Pape.

FOURME DE SALERS (also Salers)

ORIGIN	*Auvergne/cow's milk*
TYPE	*semi-firm/45% fat*
TASTE	*mellow, nutty, with a Cheddarish tang*
APPEARANCE	*tall cylinders with natural grayish-beige rind, semi-firm interior of light yellow-orange*
AVAILABILITY	*limited export*

Fourme de Salers is a mountain cheese, similar to CANTAL, produced on farms in the upland pastures in the Auvergne. One of the *appellation controlée* cheeses of France, its name is protected by law. Salers is an excellent eating cheese with wholesome, lactic flavors and good depth of character, especially in well-aged versions ripened six months or more. It keeps well and is excellent with mature full-bodied red wines such as Napa Gamay or Beaujolais.

FROMAGE DES PYRÉNÉES

A generic term that denotes any of several cow or sheep cheeses made in the Pyrénées, such as DOUX DE MONTAGNE, Pain de Pyrénées, TOMME DE PYRÉNÉES, or TOURTON (Chiberta).

FROMAGE FONDU

This is the generic term for French processed cheeses, which are generally foil-wrapped and often flavored with seasonings such as garlic, herbs and spices, nuts, cherry juice. *Fondu au Raisin,* mild and bland like most of these cheeses, is encrusted with dried grape seeds. *Gourmandise* is flavored with hazelnut and cherry. *Rambol* is often garnished with walnuts. Other brands are *Beau Pasteur, La Vache Qui Rit,* and *Reybier.* Most are based on Gruyère or other Swiss-like cheeses and processing gives them long shelf life. These are primarily snack cheeses and are popular with children.

FROMAGE FRAIS

The French term for fresh, unripened cheese. *Fromage Frais* is rich and creamy like Cream Cheese but is often more tart or sour than American Cream Cheese. It is sometimes enriched with cream, bringing the butterfat up to 60% and 75%, the levels for double and triple creams such as PETIT-SUISSE or FONTAINEBLEAU. They are best consumed as fresh as possible and are often mixed with sugar and fresh or preserved fruit.

GAPERON

ORIGIN	*Auvergne/cow' milk*
TYPE	*semi-soft/30% fat*
TASTE	*rich, spicy with garlic*
APPEARANCE	*orange-sized balls tied with ribbon; dark natural rind; ivory interior*
AVAILABILITY	*limited export*

Gaperon is a country cheese made from skimmed milk or buttermilk and flavored strongly with garlic. A fine snack or picnic cheese, it goes especially well with rough-textured breads, fresh fruit, and sturdy, simple wines such as Côte du Rhône, Petite Sirah, or Zinfandel.

GÉANT DU POITOU

ORIGIN	*Poitou/goat's milk*
TYPE	*chèvres, soft/45% fat*
TASTE	*creamy, tangy, very rich*
APPEARANCE	*9-inch flat wheels with bloomy rind; white interior*
AVAILABILITY	*limited export*

One of the more luscious-textured *chèvres,* Géant du Poitou becomes as creamy as Brie when fully ripe but retains the tart tang of goat's milk. Often mixed with cow's milk, it is not as sharp as pure goat cheeses, but it is distinctive. Excellent with dry, full-bodied whites such as Chablis, Chassagne-Montrachet, or Chardonnay.

GÉROMÉ (also Munster Géromé)

ORIGIN	*Lorraine/cow's milk*
TYPE	*monastery, semi-soft/45% fat*
TASTE	*strong, spicy*
APPEARANCE	*small to medium-sized flat discs with orange rind; soft, yellow paste*
AVAILABILITY	*limited export*

Strong, savory flavors that ripen to very pungent and pronounced aromas make Géromé similar to MUNSTER from Alsace. The cheese is of course milder when young, with a fruity tang, and it is sometimes flavored with anise, fennel, or cumin. The riper cheeses taste considerably better without the rind.

Flavored or unflavored, Géromé has the same uses as Munster and goes well with Alsace Gewurztraminer or Riesling.

GERVAIS

The brand-name of a fresh double cream produced in great quantity in the factories of Normandy. It is sold in flat little squares with snowy white rinds, and is widely available.

GOURMANDISE

This processed cheese is pale ivory in color and flavored with cherry juice (kirsch *eau-de-vie* in France). It is sold in cake form, sometimes adorned with nuts, or in foil-wrapped wedges. The flavor is mild and sweet.

GRATTE PAILLE

A soft-ripened triple cream with a light, yellowish rind, Gratte Paille is made in small loaf shapes in the Ile de France region. Its flavors are mild, creamy, and faintly salty.

GRUYÈRES

The generic term for French Swiss-style cheeses such as BEAUFORT, EMMENTAL, and COMTÉ. Gruyère is also the name of a Swiss-made cheese, also similar to Emmentaler.

LA CHEVRETTE

The brand name for a log-shaped CHÈVRE that is made creamier and milder with the addition of cow's milk. These popular cheeses are usually flavored with herbs, cracked pepper, or olives.

LA GRAPPE

A processed, flavored cheese covered with a dry crust of grape seeds. The seeds must be removed before eating.

L'AMI DU CHAMBERTIN

ORIGIN	*Burgundy/cow's milk*
TYPE	*monastery, soft/50% fat*
TASTE	*creamy, savory, salty*
APPEARANCE	*small, boxed rounds with orange, washed rind; soft, cream-white interior*
AVAILABILITY	*very limited export*

A favorite of the *cognoscenti*, this little cheese becomes quite strong when very ripe. It should be soft and smooth, but may have a firm chalky core in the middle—it should not be totally runny. The rind is washed in *marc*, which gives it a pleasantly pungent aroma. The cheese itself is milder than the rind's smell but still assertive. A mature Bordeaux or full-blooded Burgundy, such as Chambertin, complements it handsomely.

LANGRES

ORIGIN	*Northern Burgundy/cow's milk*
TYPE	*monastery, soft/50% fat*
TASTE	*earthy, sourish with lactic tang*
APPEARANCE	*biscuit-shaped mounds with concave tops, soft, whitish-orange rind, often paper-wrapped; soft ivory interior*
AVAILABILITY	*limited export*

Similar to EPOISSES in character, Langres has a strong aroma and rather sharp, pungent flavors. It is very agreeable in the stages from young to ripe, but when it is very ripe, verges on stinkiness. Stained paper, a darkened, shrunken rind, and an ammoniated smell are signs of overripeness or damage.

Langres is very good with crisp whites from Alsace, such as Pinot Blanc, or with full-bodied red wines.

LA VACHE QUI RIT

"The Laughing Cow" brand of processed cheese. Its base is Gruyère and it is most often seen in small, foil-wrapped cubes, occasionally in larger sizes.

LEZAY

Lezay are tangy logs of goat cheese from Poitou. They also come in trapezoidal bricks and may be coated with edible vegetable ash. Firm, smooth-textured, and chalky white, this CHÈVRE has a rich tang without being sharp or sour. Widely available and usually good value, it goes well with crisp, dry white wines like Sancerre or Sauvignon Blanc.

LINGOT

A mild CHÈVRE from the Loire Valley, Lingot is sometimes ash-coated. It has a very limited import and is somewhat uneven in quality with varying texture—soft and moist or dryish and somewhat chalky.

LINGOT D'OR

A Munster-style, washed-rind cheese from the Vosges Mountains in Alsace, Lingot d'Or comes in flat, orange rectangles. With 50% butterfat, it is a little milder and less complex in flavor than Munster. Trim the rind if it is strong-smelling. The cheese goes well with Alsace Gewurztraminer or Riesling.

LIVAROT

ORIGIN	*Normandy/cow's milk*
TYPE	*strong-smelling, monastery, soft/45% fat*
TASTE	*assertive with pungent aroma*
APPEARANCE	*small, thick cylinders with orange or reddish-brown rind and wrapped in sedge or reeds; yellow-gold soft interior*
AVAILABILITY	*limited export*

Sometimes nicknamed "the Colonel" because of the five strips of grass in which it is wrapped, Livarot is often overpoweringly scented. Cured in unvented cellars that are incomparably odorous, the cheese itself is far less aggressive on the palate than one would expect, especially if the rind is removed (preferably away from the eating atmosphere altogether). Livarot is one of France's oldest and most esteemed cheeses, with a fine and surprisingly appealing flavor and character beneath its smelly exterior.

Some like it with cold, fruity white wines, but in Normandy it is often served with Calvados, an appropriately forceful match, or with strong black coffee.

LOU PERALOU

A new Brie-style cheese produced from ewe's milk. Very creamy, it comes in seven-inch flat cylinders with bloomy rinds resembling COULOMMIERS. It is surprisingly delicate, with attractive tangy flavors and extravagantly creamy consistency, but tends to be overpriced.

MAROILLES (also Marolles)

ORIGIN	*Picardy, northern France/cow's milk*
TYPE	*strong-smelling/45–50% fat*
TASTE	*strong, similar to Livarot, potent aroma*
APPEARANCE	*flat squares, 5 inches in diameter; orange rind; soft yellow interior*
AVAILABILITY	*limited export*

One of France's oldest monastery cheeses, Maroilles was first made during the tenth century by monks near Lille in northern France. It is similar to LIVAROT and very ripe PONT L'EVÊQUE in pungency of aroma (its nickname is *Vieux Puant*, or "old stinker") and the "thunderous savor" of its flavors has long been appreciated by notable gourmands. The rind is rinsed in beer during the curing process.

Quart Maroilles is a smaller-sized version of Maroilles. *Gris de Lille* or *Vieux Lille* are aged longer and are consequently more potent. Maroilles requires sturdy reds such as Côte Rotie and Amarone or full-bodied ale.

MIMOLETTE

ORIGIN	*northern France/cow's milk*
TYPE	*semi-firm/45% fat*
TASTE	*mellow, bland, faintly nutty*
APPEARANCE	*large balls with dark rind, usually waxed; vivid orange, smooth interior*
AVAILABILITY	*general export*

Mimolette is a popular cheese that has flavors similar to Dutch EDAM or mild Cheddar, and a smooth, firm, sliceable texture. Generally mild-flavored and rather bland, the aged versions develop a more pronounced character. Mimolette is primarily a snack cheese and provides an interesting color contrast on the cheese tray. It is well-suited to light fruity or medium full-bodied red wines such as Beaujolais, Napa Gamay, or spicy Zinfandels.

MONTRACHET

A brand of CHÈVRE from the Burgundy region that comes in logs or small containers. Its flavors are attractively sourish and tangy and its texture is usually moist and creamy. Ash-coated logs tend to be firmer, drier, and a bit sharper in flavor. This cheese is best when quite fresh and it is very good with white Burgundies, such as Puligny-Montrachet or others of the Montrachet family, or with California Chardonnay; fruity reds and Port are also suitable.

MORBIER

ORIGIN	*Franche-Comté/cow's milk*
TYPE	*semi-soft/45% fat*
TASTE	*mild, smooth*
APPEARANCE	*flat wheels with grayish-brown rind; smooth ivory paste with center streak of gray ash*
AVAILABILITY	*limited export*

Morbier is one of the milder monastery cheeses. Supple in texture, with bland but pleasant flavors, it is immediately identifiable by the line of edible cinder that divides it. Originally the two layers were distinct cheeses made separately from the morning and evening milks and pressed together. Nowadays it is uniformly made from pasteurized milk.

Morbier is good with light red wines such as regional Bordeaux.

MUNSTER

ORIGIN	*Alsace/cow's milk*
TYPE	*monastery, semi-soft/45% fat*

TASTE *mild and savory to pungent*
APPEARANCE *small thick wheels with orange rind; yellow paste*
AVAILABILITY *general export*

One of the most widely imitated cheeses, Munster originated in a monastery in Alsace during the Middle Ages. Most imitations are bland and rather characterless, with the exception of German MÜNSTER, which is strong. Farm-produced Munster *(fermier)* has a distinct and assertive character and is sometimes quite potent in aroma. Its smooth, soft consistency is highly prized by cheese connoisseurs. Munster *laitier,* made in the creameries, tends to be less interesting but is nonetheless agreeable and consistent.

Young, full-flavored Munsters go well with Alsace Gewurztraminer; stronger ones are better suited to ale or well-hopped beer.

NEUFCHÂTEL

A popular and widely copied soft-ripened cheese made in Normandy, Neufchâtel may be found in various small shapes: square, brick, cylindrical, heart-shaped (COEUR DE BRAY). It is creamy, mild, and somewhat salty (American versions are sweeter). This cheese is best when fresh; some uncured versions are available in France, and it varies from 20 to 45% butterfat. Try it with black coffee as a mid-morning snack.

NIOLO

Niolo is a Corsican goat or sheep cheese from the central Niolo plateau. Cured in baskets, which leave their impression on the rind, it is sharp-flavored and firm-textured. This cheese is made on mountain farms and is only sporadically exported. Warning: Some versions have explosively fiery aftertaste.

PAVÉ DE JADIS (also Pavé Gençay)

This CHÈVRE comes from Provence in ash-covered bricks with moist, sliceable texture and moderately tangy flavors, suited to dry white Burgundies or California Chardonnay.

PELARDON DES CÉVENNES

Sold in small, sharp-flavored cylinders, this CHÈVRE hails from the Languedoc region of southern France. It is well-suited to Côte du Rhône reds.

PETIT SUISSE

A soft, cream-enriched (60–75% fat content), fresh cheese made all over France, Petit Suisse is sold either in small cylinders or in plastic containers. Mild and creamy, it is generally served with berries or other fruits and accompanied by strong coffee. *Gervais* is the best-known brand.

PIPO CREM'

ORIGIN   *Ain/cow's milk*
TYPE   *blue vein/50% fat*
TASTE   *rich, savory, but milder than most blues*
APPEARANCE   *5-pound logs; thin whitish rind; ivory interior with blue veins*
AVAILABILITY   *general export*

Pipo Crem' is milder than most blue cheeses and creamier in texture, with a salty, rich flavor. It should not be bitter or crumbly. A nice addition to the after-dinner cheese tray, Pipo Crem' is good with full-bodied reds from Burgundy.

POIVRE D'ANE

ORIGIN   *Provence/goat's milk*
TYPE   *chèvre/45% fat*
TASTE   *fresh, tangy, herby*
APPEARANCE   *sold in small discs covered with sprigs of savory*
AVAILABILITY   *limited export*

This *chèvre* is similar to BANON and comes from the same region, but it is flavored with herbs such as savory (*sariette* in French) or pepper. It is sometimes made from mixed goat's and cow's milk, sometimes from cow's milk alone. Its aromas are pleasant and herby and the paste mild, flavorful, and smooth-textured.

PONT L'EVÊQUE

ORIGIN   *Normandy/cow's milk*
TYPE   *monastery, soft/45–50% fat*
TASTE   *rich with a fruity tang, complex*
APPEARANCE   *sold in boxed, 4-inch squares with orange-gold rind, grid-marked; soft yellow interior*
AVAILABILITY   *general export*

This classic French cheese is from the famed Pays d'Auge region of Normandy and dates from the Middle Ages. Finding a perfectly ripened Pont L'Evêque is considered an achievement. *A point,* it will be plump and resilient inside the rind, oozing stickily rather than runny. It should not be dark or gummy, or bitter in aftertaste. Good ones are strong-smelling but not stinky; rich and creamy with a fruity, faintly sweet tang; slightly acid with a refreshing finish; of long-lasting flavor. They are delicious with fresh cider or assertive reds.

PORT SALUT (also Port-du-Salut)

ORIGIN   *western France/cow's milk*
TYPE   *monastery, semi-soft/50% fat*
TASTE   *smooth and savory*
APPEARANCE   *thick cylinders 9 inches in diameter; orange rind; smooth yellow interior*
AVAILABILITY   *general export*

Widely popular for its mouth-melting texture and savory flavors, Port Salut was first made by Trappist monks in Brittany in 1815. An immediate success when it hit Paris in the 1870's, it is now widely copied and produced in factories. It is similar to SAINT-PAULIN, and the two are sometimes indistinguishable when factory-made. One of the best Port-Salut, and one of the most authentic, has "S.A.F.R." (the initials of the firm that makes it) stamped on the rind.

Port Salut is one of the better mild cheeses, although lesser versions are often bland in flavor and gummy or rubbery in texture. Fresh fruit goes well with it, as do fruity red wines.

PRINCE DE NAVARRE

A sheep's milk cheese from the Pyrénées, Prince de Navarre is pale yellow with a hard, dark rind and rich, savory flavors reminiscent of good Cheddar or Parmesan. Hard enough for grating, it also serves as an after-dinner or snack cheese well-suited to full-flavored reds.

PYRAMIDE

These pyramid-shaped cones of CHÈVRE are made in Poitou and the central Loire; they are sharp in flavor, chalk-white, and sometimes have bluish gray or ash-coated rinds.

RAMBOL

A processed cheese, often covered with walnuts.

REBLOCHON

ORIGIN	*Savoie/cow's milk*
TYPE	*monastery, soft/45–50% fat*
TASTE	*creamy, savory*
APPEARANCE	*sold in small, firm discs with golden-brownish rind; light yellow paste with a few holes*
AVAILABILITY	*general export*

One of the milder monastery cheeses, Reblochon is semi-soft when young and soft and spreadable when ripe. Deeply flavorful, it is stronger than Saint-Paulin or Port Salut, but not as pungent as Pont L'Evêque or very ripe Munster. It ripens steadily, however, even when refrigerated, and can become pungent and bitter. The rind should be removed before eating. This cheese is very good with rough-textured breads and fruity reds such as Beaujolais Brouilly or rustic ones like Barbera d'Alba or Zinfandel.

RIGOTTE

Small biscuit-shaped CHÈVRES, now commonly made partially from cow's milk. Made mostly in the Auvergne, they have orangish rinds, are mild and pleasantly tangy.

ROLLOT

Rollot is an assertively flavored monastery cheese from

northern France, similar to PONT L'EVÊQUE, that comes in small, flat, round or heart-shaped discs. It should be soft and resilient but not gummy or hard. You can expect a good depth of flavor and a fruity, tangy edge in the finish. Rollot becomes very strong-smelling as it ripens, but the interior is milder. It is best matched with hearty reds or beer.

ROQUEFORT

ORIGIN	*Aveyron/ewe's milk*
TYPE	*blue vein/45% fat*
TASTE	*pungent, rich, salty, long, piquant aftertaste*
APPEARANCE	*stocky cylinders that are foil-wrapped with emblem of red sheep clearly visible; white natural rind; white paste with blue marbling*
AVAILABILITY	*general export*

Possibly the world's most celebrated cheese, Roquefort vies only with Stilton and Brie for the title "king of cheeses." It fairly well stands alone, however, as the most intense and individual of the blues. One of the oldest cheeses in existence, it was known in Roman times and referred to by Pliny the Elder. Charlemagne is said to have rejected it when it was presented to him but, upon tasting it, became an ardent fan.

Produced from the milk of sheep that graze on the high plateaus *(les causses)* of southern France near Rouergue (supplemented largely today by sheep's milk cheeses from Corsica) Roquefort is aged in the limestone caverns of Mount Combalou. Roquefort's unique flavors develop in the special air currents that move through the mountain's fissured depths. Long ago this unique atmosphere fostered the growth of a mold now known as *Penicillium roqueforti.* The cheeses, snow-white when they enter the caves, are skewered 36 times to aid the mold in its development and left to ripen at least three months. The rind is regularly scraped and the finished cheese wrapped in foil for shipping.

Roquefort is strictly protected and regulated by *appellation controlée* laws. No one may legally use the name or even the term "Roquefort-style." The red sheep emblem on the foil wrapper is assurance of authenticity.

Sublimely intense at its best, Roquefort should be rich and creamy-textured rather than crumbly, and not overly salty (as many exported Roqueforts are, unfortunately). Use it with a little fresh butter if you find it too powerful, although purists will eschew this practice. Roquefort overwhelms most wines, red or white, but it is a superb match for fine Sauternes (the best Roquefort and Chateau Yquem make a stunning contrast). It may also provide an opportunity to serve those powerful, late-harvest Zinfandels or Zin Essence.

ROYAL PROVENCE

This is a mild, creamy CHÈVRE made into small white wheels, and flavored with pepper or crowned with sliced olives. It is not as tangy as some goat cheese because of the addition of cow's milk, but is quite popular.

SAINT ANDRÉ

A widely-produced TRIPLE CREAM, beguilingly rich and luscious but lacking in character after the initial impact of richness.

SAINT CHRISTOPHE

CHÈVRE from the Loire Valley, Saint Christophe has a white rind or is ash-coated and is sold in the shape of a small log.

SAINT FLORENTIN

ORIGIN	*Yonne/cow's milk*
TYPE	*soft/45% fat*
TASTE	*tangy, spicy, piquant*
APPEARANCE	*loose white curds, very moist; sold in containers*
AVAILABILITY	*very limited import*

Some cheese books refer to this cheese as a soft-ripened variety similar to Epoisses, but today's exports are fresh, unripened cheeses with a salty tang—occasionally they are so fresh that they are still dripping with whey. In this state, the cheese, which is perishable to begin with, sours quickly, so examine each container carefully before you buy. It is a good spread on pumpernickel bread or bagels, with black coffee.

SAINT MARCELLIN

ORIGIN	*Isère/goat's milk, cow's milk*
TYPE	*chèvre, soft/45% fat*
TASTE	*fresh, creamy, piquant*
APPEARANCE	*sold in small white discs; chalk-white interior*
AVAILABILITY	*limited export*

Once made of pure goat's milk on farms in eastern France, today Saint Marcellin is often only 50% goat's milk and the rest cow's milk. According to some authorities, Saint Marcellin is now all cow's milk, but its piquant tang and soft, moist texture suggest that a fair amount of goat's milk remains. It is often confused with BANON, but Banon is firmer in texture and may contain even less goat's milk.

Saint Marcellin also comes in small jars mixed with olive oil and herbs and is then referred to as *Le Pitchou*. But treatment with olive oil and herbs is one you can do yourself with a less heavy-handed effect (see page 38).

SAINTE MAURE

ORIGIN *Touraine/goat's milk*
TYPE *chèvres/45% fat*
TASTE *fresh, mild to piquant*
APPEARANCE *log-shaped, bluish or downy white rind, smooth white interior*
AVAILABILITY *general export*

One of the most popular *chèvres* from the Loire Valley, Sainte Maure is also made in Anjou and Poitou. Farm-produced goat cheeses of this name have natural bluish-gray rinds flecked with dark brown, whereas factory versions have bloomy rinds and develop a creamier consistency when ripe. Both are tangy and piquant, excellent with Loire Valley whites such as Sancerre or Pouilly-Fumé, Vouvray *sec,* or Loire reds.

SAINT NECTAIRE

ORIGIN *Auvergne/cow's milk*
TYPE *semi-soft/45% fat*
TASTE *mild, savory, tangy finish*
APPEARANCE *flat, thick wheels, eight inches in diameter, natural, light orange rind with some white-ish mold; pale yellow interior*
AVAILABILITY *general export*

This is one of the better semi-soft cheeses, similar to Saint Paulin but fruitier, with an appealing tang and a certain nuttiness of flavor. An old cheese, dating at least to the Middle Ages, it has long been popular in France as well as in export markets.

Saint Nectaire is a good choice for providing contrast on the cheese board. It is good with most reds, particularly fruity ones such as Beaujolais Brouilly, Fleurie or Chiroubles, light Burgundies like Mercurey, or California Pinot Noir.

SAINT PAULIN

ORIGIN *France/cow's milk*
TYPE *monastery, semi-soft/45% fat*
TASTE *mild, savory*
APPEARANCE *thick wheels, nine inches in diameter, thin orange rind; smooth, light yellow interior*
AVAILABILITY *general export*

Saint Paulin is a semi-soft monastery cheese modeled after the original Port-du-Salut. Produced in factories in Brittany, Maine, Anjou, and elsewhere, it is sometimes more bland in character than Port-du-Salut but is nevertheless an agreeable cheese that slices easily for snacks or sandwiches. Bonbel is the most common brand. Préclos and others from Brittany seem to have more robust flavor and character.

Like Port-du-Salut, it keeps very well when snugly wrapped in plastic and refrigerated. It is most suitable to fruity red wines, white wines, and beer.

ST. SAVIOL

Trade name for several good and reasonably consistent goat cheeses (CHÈVRES) produced in the western Loire.

SARRAZIN

Sarrazin is sold in flat wheels and has an orange washed rind and semi-soft yellow interior. It is similar to CHAUMES but is supple and more pliable in texture rather than soft. It is full-flavored and strong in aroma when fully ripe. Sarrazin is generally only available domestically, although it is occasionally exported.

SELLES-SUR-CHER

ORIGIN	*Touraine/goat's milk*
TYPE	*chèvres/45% fat*
TASTE	*bland to quite piquant*
APPEARANCE	*sold in flat-topped cones or cylinders, bloomy rind, some coated with cinders; chalk-white paste*
AVAILABILITY	*very limited export*

Selles is a small town near Tours on the River Cher, a tributary of the Loire. This little goat cheese can be excellent, with a mildly piquant, goaty character and a dryish, chalky texture. Exports vary considerably, however; some are quite bland, others are overripe and excessively pungent, with darkened interiors and tough rinds. Look for the Jacquin label, and buy only the freshest specimens.

Serve Selles-sur-Cher with fresh fruit and crisp white or fruity red wines.

SOUMAINTRAIN

This soft-ripened cheese from northern Burgundy is similar to LANGRES but yellower in color. When very ripe, Soumaintrain, which is not often exported, develops a crusty orange rind and flavor akin to Munster in full bloom.

SUPRÊME

The brand name for one of Normandy's soft-ripened DOUBLE CREAMS.

TAUPINIÈRE

A dome-shaped *chèvre* from the Loire Valley with a black-and-white bloomy rind, Taupinière has dry, tangy, and austerely musty flavors that grow sharper with age. The texture is moist, smooth, and firm, but gets drier as it ages. Taupinière is not heavily exported, but may be found in specialty shops. It is excellent with Sancerre.

TOMME

This term generally refers to semi-firm or semi-soft mountain cheeses of rather simple character, such as those from the

Pyrénées or Savoie. But in some rural regions it simply means "cheese" and is used for many different types, such as *Tommes Arlsienne,* a soft ewe's milk cheese, and several farm-made goat cheeses from southern and eastern France.

TOMME DE SAVOIE

ORIGIN	*Savoie/cow's milk*
TYPE	*semi-soft/45% fat*
TASTE	*mildly savory, nutty*
APPEARANCE	*thick wheels, eight inches in diameter; ochre rind with whitish mold; yellow paste, few holes*
AVAILABILITY	*general export*

One of the better mountain cheeses, *Tomme de Savoie* is somewhat similar to Saint Nectaire, with attractive nutty flavors and fruity fragrance. It keeps well if securely wrapped and refrigerated, but the aroma gets stronger with age—trimming the rind helps since the cheese inside rarely moves past mild savoriness.

This cheese is quite nice with sturdy, fruity reds like Morgon, Mercurey, and Crozes-Hermitage.

TOMME DES PYRÉNÉES

Tommes des Pyrénées are medium-sized cylinders or wheels of semi-soft cheese with hard, sometimes waxed, rinds that are produced in the Pyrénées region of southwestern France. Most are quite bland and without much character, although they are pleasant enough for snacks.

TONNELAIT

This mountain-style *tommes* is in fact made on the grassy plains of Brittany from cow's milk and is sold in stocky cylinders. With its mild, smooth flavors and supple, semi-soft texture, Tonnelait is an agreeable, if not especially interesting, snack cheese.

TOURTON (formerly Chiberta)

ORIGIN	*Pyrénées/cow's milk*
TYPE	*monastery, semi-soft/45% fat*
TASTE	*mildly tangy*
APPEARANCE	*small, thick wheels; thin, orange rind; yellow paste dotted with holes*
AVAILABILITY	*general export*

Tourton is one of the typical, supple-textured cheeses in the style of Bel Paese and Saint-Paulin that are made throughout the Pyrénées region. It has a bit more tang and character than Tomme de Pyrénées or Doux de Montagne but is basically a simple cheese with a mildly pronounced aroma.

Tourton is fine as a snack cheese or for picnics, with fruity red wines.

VALEMBERT

A relatively new, factory-produced, semi-soft cheese similar to SAINT PAULIN but with a bloomy rind.

VALENCAY (also Pyramide)

ORIGIN	*Central Loire/goat's milk*
TYPE	*chèvre/45% fat*
TASTE	*tangy, sometimes quite strong*
APPEARANCE	*sold in flat-topped, pyramidal cones, either white or ash-coated; chalky white centers*
AVAILABILITY	*limited export*

Valencay is one of the sharpest *chèvres,* especially in its bluish-black, farm-produced incarnation that is pure goat's milk but tends to be seasonal. The factory versions, with their white, downy rinds, are made year-round but are also variable in quality. When young and fresh, the little pyramids are mildly piquant and quite delightful, but they get strong, musty, and ammoniated when they are too old.

Valencay is especially good with ripe plums and dry, crisp white wines of the Loire, such as Sancerre and Savennières.

VENACO

ORIGIN	*Corsica/lait de mélange*
TYPE	*semi-firm/45% fat*
TASTE	*salty, sharp, swarthy*
APPEARANCE	*comes in small, thick blocks with foil-wrapped, washed rinds; pale yellow interior, irregular holes*
AVAILABILITY	*limited export*

The term *lait de mélange,* which appears on the labels, indicates that the cheese was made from an unspecified mix of sheep's, goat's, or cow's milk. The sharp, salty tang and supple, somewhat oily, texture of most Venaco suggests that they are mostly sheep's milk. If not overly sharp, it has a vivid and appealing savoriness about it that provides an interesting contrast to other cheeses, after dinner or at a tasting. It requires sturdy reds to stand up to it.

VIEUX PANÉ

ORIGIN	*Aveyron/cow's milk*
TYPE	*semi-soft/45% fat*
TASTE	*mellow, nutty, smooth*
APPEARANCE	*large, flat squares with honey-orange, washed rind; yellow interior, few holes*
AVAILABILITY	*limited export*

Although Vieux Pané looks like a large Pont l'Evêque, its aroma and flavor are milder and sweeter, with tinges of hazelnut and a lactic acidity that gives a very clean finish. It is good with Médocs or Saint-Emilion.

◆◆◆

ITALY

ravelers to Italy discover with delight the diverse world of Italian cheese, until recently a world largely unto itself. No longer, however, are cheese-lovers confined to the harder, aged cheeses known for their keeping qualities. Air Express and specialty cheese shops now make it possible—at a price, of course—to enjoy some of Italy's delectable fresh and soft-ripened cheeses like Mascarpone, the Robiolas, Stracchino Cresczenza, Scamorze, and numerous others. The growing demand for fine cheese has also resulted in increasing export of Italy's classics—superbly aged Parmigiano-Reggiano, a variety of Gorgonzolas, the genuine and original Fontina from the Val d'Aosta, and the finest Provolone.

Many of Italy's cheeses were developed centuries ago, for cheese has been appreciated by the Italians since antiquity. Over a dozen cheeses were sold in the *velabrium* (dairy market) in ancient Rome, including varieties from Gaul, Helvetia, and even the British Isles. Legend attributes cheese-making to Romulus himself, who was said to have made Pecorino about the time he and his brother founded Rome. Argricultural writers of the Augustan Age were full of cheese-making tips. Columella advised using extracts of thistle, saf-flower, and fig bark as curdling agents. He also suggested pine seeds as a kind of rennet for goat's milk cheese. In *De Agricultura,* the oldest surviving Latin book of any kind, Cato provided recipes for cheese pastries called *Libum* and *Placcenta,* probably made with a kind of Ricotta. By the Renaissance, many modern cheese types were well estab-lished and were an important part of Italian cuisine. When

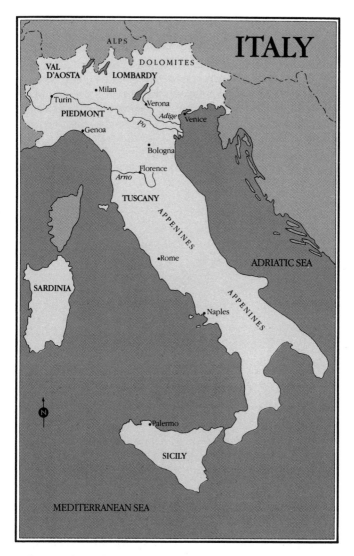

Catherine di Medici departed for France in the mid-sixteenth century, the glory of Tuscan cuisine, with its liberal use of Parmesan, went with her.

Italians appear to make cheeses from a greater variety of animal sources—and in a greater variety of ways—than any other people in the world. They use the milk of cows, goats, and sheep; some say Caciocavallo was once made of mare's milk. Water buffalo from the East were imported in the seventh century and vast herds of their descendants still graze in the marshes of Campania in order to supply the milk for Mozzarella and Scamorze. Cheeses are stretched and shaped into everything from egg-shaped balls to figures of saints and little pigs. They are whipped like cream, solidified into a soft mass by heating the whey, impregnated with mold, and ripened to a pliant consistency that is neither too soft nor too hard.

The great variety of Italian cheese is due in part to the land-scape. Most of the rich cow's milk cheeses come from the fertile northern basin between the Alps and the Apennines, covering much of the Piedmont, Lombardy, and the Veneto. The smaller and more hilly central regions of Latium around Rome and Naples are the home of the *pasta filata* (plastic curd) cheeses like Mozzarella, as well as numerous goat and sheep cheeses. Southernmost, mountainous Sicily is the originator of many sheep cheeses and of the whey cheese, Ricotta.

Cheese Guide

ANNABELLA

ORIGIN *Piedmont/cow's milk*
TYPE *fresh/40–45% fat*
TASTE *mild, creamy*
APPEARANCE *soft, white, rindless cheese packed in square wooden boxes*
AVAILABILITY *limited export*

This *fresco formaggio,* or "fresh cheese," is similar to the milk-white cream cheeses made for early consumption. At the peak of freshness, it is mild creamy, rich but delicate, and very spreadable. Somewhat similar to fresh ROBIOLA, Annabella makes a lovely brunch or luncheon cheese and is excellent with crisp, white wines such as Pinot Bianco, Pinot Grigio, or Sauvignon Blanc. It is also superb with preserved fruit and black coffee.

ASIAGO

ORIGIN *Vicenza/cow's milk*
TYPE *semi-firm/30–45% fat*
TASTE *rich and nutty to sharp and piquant*
APPEARANCE *small wheels with flat sides; glossy rind, yellow interior with small eyes*
AVAILABILITY *general export*

Asiago, made principally in Vicenza, but also in other parts of the Veneto and Lombardy, is either a Cheddar-like table cheese or a grating cheese, depending on age. Aged up to a year, it is a fine eating cheese, with the nutty richness and sharp tang of Cheddar. At this age, it is a good companion for fruity reds such as Barbera d'Alba, California Zinfandel, or Petite Sirah.

Older cheeses aged up to two years become hard and brittle, suitable for grating. The sharper, aged Asiago can also be an after-dinner or snack cheese; it needs a brawnier red wine, however, such as Barbaresco or Barolo. Most Asiago is made from partially skimmed milk, but Asiago *grasso di monte,* a full-cream version aged six weeks, is sometimes found locally.

When buying Asiago look for even color throughout. There should be no dark spots in the paste or cracks in the rind. Asiago for grating should have a fine granular texture similar to Parmesan. Asiago keeps well in the refrigerator if it is wrapped securely in plastic wrap. It melts easily and is often used in cooking.

BEL PAESE

ORIGIN	*Lombardy/cow's milk*
TYPE	*semi-soft/50% fat*
TASTE	*mild, creamy, fruity*
APPEARANCE	*thick, foil-wrapped discs; pale interior with small irregular holes; sold in wedges*
AVAILABILITY	*widely exported, also produced in the U.S.*

Bel Paese (the name means "beautiful country") is one of the world's most popular cheeses. Dependably consistent in quality, its mild but distinctive character makes it useful for snacks, sandwiches, or as a contrast to stronger cheeses on the cheese board. It is a fairly new cheese, developed in the 1920's by one Egidio Galbani, who wanted to make a soft cheese similar to French *Saint-Paulin.* It was modeled to some extent after FIORE DI ALPE, a mild, soft-textured cheese made in the Val d'Aosta.

Bel Paese is an ideal mild cheese for both producer and consumer. It ripens quickly, within four to eight weeks. Its creamy smooth texture and faint sweetness make it delicious with fruity white wines, rosés, or light reds. It melts easily and makes a flavorful topping for casseroles, soups, and even pizza.

A reasonably good imitation of Bel Paese is also produced in the United States, although it is somewhat blander and sometimes slightly bitter, as the best Italian cheese never is. The two versions have similar wrappings. Both show a priest (Father Stoppani, who wrote a popular children's book called *Bel Paese,* is on the Italian wrapper) and a map. But the imported version has a map of Italy, whereas the American version shows a map of North and South America.

BRIGANTE

ORIGIN	*Sardinia/sheep's milk*
TYPE	*semi-firm/45% fat*
TASTE	*tangy, salty*
APPEARANCE	*thick cylinders with grooved black rind, off-white interior, few holes*
AVAILABILITY	*limited export*

A semi-firm sheep's milk cheese from Sardinia. Savory and rich with a sheepy tang, it has a supple, smooth texture and can be hard enough for grating.

CACIOCAVALLO

ORIGIN	*Campania/cow's milk*
TYPE	*pasta filata/45% fat*
TASTE	*mild but tangy, sharper with age*
APPEARANCE	*pear- or gourd-shaped; glossy, yellow-gold rind; semi-firm ivory interior*
AVAILABILITY	*general export*

Pasta filata are drawn-curd cheeses made in a special way. The curds are bathed in hot whey until they become elastic. They are then stretched and shaped by hand; other *pasta filata* cheeses are Provolone and Mozzarella. Caciocavallo is an old cheese, dating at least to the fourteenth century, probably earlier. It is believed to have been brought to Italy from the eastern Mediterranean, for it resembles such cheeses as Bulgarian KASHKAVAL, Turkish KASAR PEYNIR, and others of Balkan origin. When aged about four months, it tastes somewhat like a young Cheddar, with a similar close, flaky texture, but more tang and bite. Aged longer it becomes sharper, more granular in texture, and very hard and is often used for grating.

The name is derived from *cacio a cavallo*—"cheese on horseback"—and suggests to some that it may originally have been made from mare's milk. More likely the name comes from the fact that, traditionally, two cheeses were tied together for drying and slung across a pole, saddle-bag style. The name may also refer to the symbol of the city of Naples—a galloping horseman—that was sometimes represented on the exterior. Caciocavallo keeps well if snugly wrapped and refrigerated. Correctly made, it will not be bitter or overly sharp. It goes very well with the wines of Tuscany, such as Chianti Riserva.

CACIOTTA

Caciotta means "little cheese" and is a general designation for small cheeses made on farms in several regions. *Caciotta di Lodi,* from Lombardy, is a young, perishable cheese made from cow's milk, that is mild, creamy, and faintly sour. *Caciotta altopascio* from Tuscany, made from a mixture of cow's and sheep's milk, is stronger and firmer in texture.

Caciotta di Siena is made from sheep's milk and is richer and quite good. (However, watch out for overly ammoniated ones.) Others are made from goat's milk, and most have hard, natural rinds that often show mold. Younger ones are semi-soft, moist, and rather mild, but they become firmer and more pungent as they ripen.

CAPRINO (also Caprini)

ORIGIN	*northern Italy/goat's milk, cow's milk*
TYPE	*fresh/40–45% fat*
TASTE	*mild, creamy with pleasant tang*
APPEARANCE	*soft, white interior like cream cheese; sold in wooden boxes or 5- to 6-inch paper-wrapped cylinders*
AVAILABILITY	*mostly local, limited export*

Caprino is a creamy, mild, fresh cheese, now mostly made from cow's milk, with an appealing tang or sourness. It is delicious with fresh fruit, fruit preserves, or with crudités, fresh tomatoes, olives, and dry white or fruity red wines. It is best when very fresh and moist, the *raison d'être* for this type of cheese. (Do not confuse Caprino with *Caprino Romano,* a hard grating cheese of the family PECORINO ROMANO.)

CRESCENZA (also Crescenza Stracchino)

ORIGIN	*Lombardy, Piedmont, Veneto/cow's milk*
TYPE	*fresh/50%+ fat*
TASTE	*delicate, creamy, mildly tart*
APPEARANCE	*soft-textured, ivory-yellow interior; sold in wooden boxes*
AVAILABILITY	*limited export*

One of the most popular of the fresh, uncooked STRACCHINO cheeses. Ripe in ten days to two weeks, it is very perishable and does not travel well. Air Express, however, makes limited quantities available in export markets, and its delicious creaminess makes it a hot item at specialty cheese shops. Be sure it is fresh, moist, and plump when you buy, and eat it soon after purchase. At room temperature it becomes butter-soft and is, in fact, used like butter on its home ground in northern Italy.

CROTONESE

ORIGIN	*Calabria, Sicily/sheep's milk*
TYPE	*hard, Grana/32% fat*
TASTE	*sharp*
APPEARANCE	*small thick cylinders with tough natural rind; pale ochre, dense, granular interior*
AVAILABILITY	*limited export*

This hard, Grana-style cheese of southern Italy has the sharp piquancy of a cheese made from sheep's milk, especially when it is mixed with goat's milk, as Crotonese sometimes is.

I'm told that in Sicily it is ripened with the aid of a certain species of worms and it is purchased only when the worms are alive and moving inside the cheese; imported versions however show no evidence of this.

DOLCE LATTE (also Dolcelatte)

The brand name of one of the milder, factory-made GORGONZOLAS.

DOLCEZZA

A fresh, skimmed-milk cheese with the texture and delicacy of sweet butter. It is rarely seen outside Italy and can be rather flavorless.

FIOR D'ALPE

ORIGIN	*Lombardy/cow's milk*
TYPE	*semi-soft/50% fat*
TASTE	*mild and bland*
APPEARANCE	*smooth, elastic texture, pale color*
AVAILABILITY	*mostly local*

Similar to BEL PAESE, which was modeled after it, Fior d'Alpe is a pleasant enough snack or sandwich cheese. It slices easily but is not as flavorful as Bel Paese. The name means "flower of the alps."

FIORE SARDO

ORIGIN	*Sardinia/sheep's milk*
TYPE	*hard/45% fat*
TASTE	*rich, full-flavored, sharp when aged*
APPEARANCE	*thick wheels with yellow rind, pale yellow interior*
AVAILABILITY	*limited export*

This Sardinian *pecorino* (or sheep's milk cheese) is a good table cheese when young, aged about two months or so, but it is more highly prized as a grating cheese, for the piquancy it adds to various dishes. It is often used in combination with grated Paramesan. For the younger version, which you will most likely encounter on Sardinia or in and around Rome, pick a robust Italian red such as Rubesco di Torgiano.

FONTINA VAL D'AOSTA (also Fontina Valdostana)

ORIGIN	*Piedmont/cow's milk*
TYPE	*semi-firm/45% fat*
TASTE	*nutty, delicately rich*
APPEARANCE	*dark gold, crusty rind; pale gold interior, scattered small holes*
AVAILABILITY	*limited export*

The original and authentic Fontina made in the Val d'Aosta of the northern Piedmont, is so unlike most cheeses sold as Fontina that one wonders how the imitators ever came to use the name. The rich, but subtly distinctive flavor and firm, dense texture of the original are unique. (Look for the cooperative trademark stamped in purple on the rind.) Made from the milk of cows that graze high on the sub-alpine slopes, mature Fontina has a dry, slightly austere, but earthy character. A hint of white truffle (native to the Piedmont) is noticeable in mature Fontinas aged four months or more. Younger versions are less pronounced in character but still excellent after-dinner cheeses, well served by one of the balanced Nebbiolo wines such as Gattinara, Carema, or Inferno.

Fontinas made elsewhere in Italy (often called *Fontinella*) and throughout the world (Denmark, France, United States, Sweden) are made from pasteurized milk. While they can be quite good, they lack the depth of character of genuine Fontina. They are softer in texture, bland or strong-flavored depending on age, and tend to be more similar to one another than to the original Fontina Val d'Aosta. Still, they are pleasant (if not too rubbery in texture), and widely available.

FORMAGELLE D'ARTAVAGGIO

ORIGIN	*Lombardy/cow's milk*
TYPE	*soft-ripened/48% fat*
TASTE	*mild, creamy, salty*
APPEARANCE	*small thick cylinders; sticky rind; creamy, yellow interior*
AVAILABILITY	*limited export*

A washed-rind cheese traditionally ripened in the caves of Sassina near Como in Lombardy, Formagelle d'Artavaggio is mild but savory when fresh. As it ripens, its saltiness becomes concentrated, and within a few weeks it verges on stinkiness, the stage at which some cheese-lovers find it glorious.

FORMAGGIO

The Italian term for cheese.

FORMAGGIO GRANDUCA

A rich, luscious triple cream, gorgeously full-flavored in its native territory (northern and northwestern Italy). Some exported versions are oddly flavorless, however. Exports are very limited; sample before buying, if possible.

GORGONZOLA

ORIGIN	*Lombardy/cow's milk*
TYPE	*blue vein/48% fat*
TASTE	*rich, savory, pungent*
APPEARANCE	*thick, foil-wrapped wheels; white or ivory interior with blue-green veining*
AVAILABILITY	*general export*

One of Italy's finest cheeses and one of the world's most distinguished blues, Gorgonzola ranks with Roquefort and Stilton, but is creamier than either. Its veins, formed by the *Penicillium glaucum* mold, first developed when the cheese was aged for long months in caves outside the little town of Gorgonzola near Milan; they are more greenish than blue in color. Gorgonzola can be one of the most pungent and strong-flavored of the blues—spicy, piquant, with the earthy touch of the barnyard or dank cavern about it. As a result of today's economics and palates, curing times have been reduced to around six months, sometimes less, so that the cheeses are milder. White Gorgonzola (also called *Pannarone*) has no mold. *Dolcelatte,* a factory-made Gorgonzola, is white and mild with light veining. Aged Gorgonzola has very heavy mold and is quite strong and sharp; it is also drier and more crumbly than younger versions.

Gorgonzola calls for robust red wines like Barolo, Barbaresco, Amarone, or perhaps late-harvest Zinfandel. Mild to medium Gorgonzola is superb with fresh pears or peaches. Sometimes it is mixed with Mascarpone or herbs, as in TORTA CON BASILICO which consists of layers of Gorgonzola alternating with layers of basil. It adds zest when crumbled into salads or melted over potatoes or steak.

GRANA PADANO

ORIGIN	*Lombardy/cow's milk*
TYPE	*hard, Grana/32% fat*
TASTE	*similar to Parmesan but more delicate*
APPEARANCE	*medium-large cylinders; rough, brownish, natural hard rind; yellow-gold, flaky-textured interior*
AVAILABILITY	*limited export*

Grana means "grain" and refers to the grainy texture of this Parmesan-like cheese, made in several parts of the Piedmont as well as in Lombardy. It can be excellent, both as an eating cheese and as a grating cheese. However, its production is not as strictly controlled as that of PARMIGIANO-REGGIANO, so the quality varies, depending on the season, the region, the producer, and the quality of the milk. While Parmigiano is usually aged at least two years, Grana Padano is often sold after a year. The younger cheeses are better for table use and are best accompanied by sturdy reds such as Grumello,

Sassella, or Inferno of the Valtellina or Nebbiolo d'Alba of the Piedmont.

Other regional Granas are Grana Lodigiano (made near Lodi) or Grana Lombardo.

GRUVIERA (also Groviera)

The Italian version of Swiss GRUYÈRE, produced mostly in Lombardy and Piedmont. Quite good.

MANTECA (also Burrino)

A *pasta filata* cheese, usually Mozzarella, that has a ball of sweet butter in its center. Manteca is very popular in many parts of Italy, especially the South where it was a useful way to store butter. Sometimes lightly smoked Caciocavallo is used. Sliced open, the smooth white cheese (with a darkened rind if smoked) makes an appealing contrast to the pale yellow knob of butter in the center. Usually the butter is scooped out, spread on a piece of bread, and then topped with a slice of cheese. It is well-suited to dry white wines or fruity reds and rosés.

MASCARPONE (also Mascherpone)

ORIGIN	*Lombardy/cow's milk*
TYPE	*fresh, double cream/60% fat*
TASTE	*rich, buttery, slightly acidic*
APPEARANCE	*soft, pale ivory mass, sold in containers*
AVAILABILITY	*limited export*

This fresh, delicate cheese, now made all over Italy has been likened to the clotted cream known in England as Devonshire. Sometimes it is as light as whipped cream; at other times it has the consistency and delicate flavor of sweet butter, for which it is occasionally substituted. It can be lovely with fresh, ripe pears, or topped with fresh strawberries and Strega or brandy. It is quite versatile, however, and in the northeastern district of Friuli, it is often mixed with anchovies, mustard, and spices. It may also be mixed with Gorgonzola or spread between layers of Provolone.

It is very perishable and usually sells out quickly, so get to know your cheese vendor to find out exactly when it will be available.

MONCENISIO

A mild, white GORGONZOLA with a light veining of blue mold, made in the Savoy mountains of western Piedmont.

MONTASIO

A table or grating cheese similar to *Asiago* but closer to Swiss *Emmentaler* in flavor and texture, Montasio hardens with age and is then mostly used for grating.

MOZZARELLA

ORIGIN *Italy/buffalo's or cow's milk*
TYPE *pasta filata/40–45% fat*
TASTE *mild, delicate, sometimes smoked*
APPEARANCE *varies—balls, ovals, rectangles, pear-shaped*
AVAILABILITY *limited export*

An Italian original, Mozzarella is most famous in the United States as the "pizza cheese." It is one of Italy's *pasta filata* cheeses, which during production are dipped in hot whey and kneaded to the proper consistency. A fresh, mild, white cheese (yellowing is a bad sign) Mozzarella is most highly prized in Italy when it is fresh, even hours old. It is then sliced, sprinkled with olive oil, salt, and cracked pepper, and served on fresh white bread. The best is made from the milk of the water buffalo that were brought to Italy centuries ago. (Herds still graze on the plains of Campania and elsewhere.) Fresh Mozzarella from cow's milk is also good and is made daily in the Italian sections of many cities. It is delightful served with fresh tomatoes, anchovies, black olives, and dry white wines or rosés. *Mozzarella Affumicata* is lightly smoked and delectable, especially as an extra flavor-note in salads. MANTECA is Mozzarella with a knot of sweet butter implanted in the middle. *Boconccini* are little balls of buffalo-milk Mozzarella.

The delicate flavors of young Mozzarella won't keep beyond a week, so the fresher, the better. Supermarket varieties can be rubbery, flavorless, or overly salty and are better used for cooking. SCAMORZE is dried Mozzarella; it is firmer in texture, mildly salty, and quite tasty.

Mozzarella in Carozza
("Mozzarella in a Carriage")

Sliced Mozzarella Cheese
1 *loaf medium-size of French or Italian bread*
1 *cup of milk*
1 *cup of breadcrumbs*
¼ *cup of milk beaten together with*
3 *eggs*
Vegetable oil for deep frying

Slice the loaf horizontally, cut into 3-inch sections and put slices of Mozzarella between each slice. Dip the sandwich in the milk, roll in the breadcrumbs then dip in the milk and egg mixture. Deep fry until slightly brown and crisp. Serve very hot.

Anchovies or Proscuitto may be added to the sandwich if desired.

PAGLIETTA

Sold in small, flat discs, Paglietta is a soft-ripened cheese made from cow's milk in northern Italy. It is creamy ivory in color, with a soft, pliant, almost Brie-like texture. It is mildly rich with a faint ammonia scent from the surface mold and an excellent cheese when exactly, but not overly, ripe. Its fragility makes for very limited export and it is available only in specialty cheese shops.

PANNARONE (also Gorgonzola bianca)

Fresh, white GORGONZOLA without the blue mold, Pannarone is tangy and slightly sharp and is found mostly in Lombardy. The name comes from *panna,* the Italian word for cream.

PARMIGIANO-REGGIANO (also Parmesan)

ORIGIN	*Emilia-Romagna/cow's milk*
TYPE	*hard, Grana/32–35% fat*
TASTE	*rich, spicy, sharp, but not biting*
APPEARANCE	*large cylinders (up to 75 pounds); oily, golden, hard rind; golden granular interior, sometimes crystalline*
AVAILABILITY	*general export*

One of Italy's oldest cheeses, said to have evolved from an ancient Etruscan recipe, Parmigiano-Reggiano is one of the world's most famous and widely imitated cheeses. Although other Grana cheeses, such as Grana Padano, are similar and nearly as good, none equal its quality. It is known mostly as a grating cheese (what would pasta be without it?) and its subtle spiciness has enhanced and ennobled Italian dishes since the Renaissance. The making of Parmigiano is strictly controlled and it is aged with care like a fine wine.

Cheeses with the name Parmigiano-Reggiano stencilled on the rind are produced only in a designated area that includes Parma (whence its name), Modena, Mantua, and Bologna. It is produced only from mid-April to mid-November—never from winter milk—and aged at least 14 months, more commonly two years. *Stravecchio* is aged three years, *Stravecchione,* four years and sometimes the date is stamped on the rind. Its subtle richness, depth of flavor, and complex character combine for a pleasing sharpness without bitterness or bite in the aftertaste. Older cheeses develop tiny white crystals that are almost crunchy in texture yet melt quickly in the mouth. Younger cheeses are fine for after dinner, accompanied by fresh fruit and full-bodied red wines like Rubesco, Vino Nobile, Brunello di Montalcino, Taurasi, or similar robust wines.

Properly aged Parmesan is goldish-yellow; whitish ones may be too young and lacking in character. Look for an unbroken rind and evenly granulated texture when you buy. Sample if possible—good Parmigiano should not be bitter or too salty.

Parmesan cheeses are also made in Argentina, Australia, and the United States. The Wisconsin-made Stella brand is the most commendable American version for grating.

PASTA FILATA

The term literally means "spun paste" and refers to plastic or stretched-curd cheeses such as Mozzarella, Provolone, Caciocavallo, and others. When they are made, they are covered in hot whey, then stretched or kneaded to a plastic consistency that can be molded or shaped.

PECORINO ROMANO

ORIGIN	*central, southern Italy/sheep's milk*
TYPE	*hard, Grana/35% fat*
TASTE	*sharp with sheepy tang*
APPEARANCE	*large cylinders with hard, yellowish rind; light yellow interior*
AVAILABILITY	*general export*

All sheep's milk cheeses are known as *pecorino* in Italy. This one, made mostly in Latium, is best known as a hard, sharply piquant grating cheese. Young Pecorino Romano, known as *Ricotta Pecorino,* is white, soft, moist, and mild, but still flavorful, with an appealing "sheepy" tang. Rindless, it keeps well snugly wrapped and refrigerated; although it becomes drier, it doesn't lose its flavor.

Aged Pecorino Romano is hard, sometimes quite brittle, and sharper than other grating cheeses. It should not, however, be bitter or overly granular in texture. It is good with sausages, cured olives, rough-textured bread, and robust red wines. Sometimes mistaken for Parmesan when pre-grated, Pecorino Romano is a perfectly acceptable substitute; in fact, its extra tang is sometimes preferred over Parmesan. *Pecorino Siciliano* and *Pecorino Sardo* come from Sicily and Sardinia. *Pecorino Romano* is the oldest and considered the best.

PROVATURA ROMANA

Provatura Romano refers to small cheeses similar to Mozzarella and made from the milk of the water buffalo. They are sold in egg-shaped spheres in and around Rome. Fresh and perishable, they are generally only available locally, although some are exported to specialty shops.

PROVOLONE

ORIGIN	*Campania, southern Italy/cow's milk*
TYPE	*pasta filata/about 45% fat*
TASTE	*mild to sharp, depending on age*
APPEARANCE	*sold in various shapes (salami, pear, cone, cylinder); gold to light brown glossy rind; whitish-yellow interior*
AVAILABILITY	*general export*

Walk into an Italian delicatessen anywhere in the world and you're likely to be greeted by the sight of Provolone cheeses suspended from the rafters in all shapes and sizes, from the huge salami shapes that weigh up to 200 pounds to plump little piglets, all hand-molded.

Like Cheddar, Provolone sharpens with age. *Dolce,* aged about two months, is the mildest, with a smooth, even texture, and makes a good sandwich cheese. *Piccante* is aged four to six months, and some of the larger Provolones are aged a year or more. In the older cheeses the flavors are much more pronounced and have a bit of bite; the color is richer, and the texture often is flaky. The ripest ones are grainy and suitable for grating. Provolone is a good cooking cheese; you can stuff *ravioli* or *canneloni* with it or melt it on top of meat or bread. Sometimes smoked, it is a notable companion to ham and good Chianti Riserva.

One of the best brands of Provolone, known for being fine and well-aged, is *Auricchio,* not to be confused with a domestic brand of this name. The name or an "A" is stamped on the rind. It is also more expensive. Some Provolone Dolce is sold in logs, rolled with layers of prosciutto; these are ideal for salads or picnics and can be delicious for snacks with beer or light wines.

QUARTIROLO

A mild, semi-soft cheese made in Lombardy from spring and summer milk, Quartirolo is similar in appearance to BEL PAESE but is sold in small rectangles.

RICOTTA

ORIGIN	*all Italy, especially Sicily/cow's milk*
TYPE	*fresh, whey/4–10% fat*
TASTE	*mild, fresh, and sweetish*
APPEARANCE	*white, fluffy or smooth interior; packed in containers*
AVAILABILITY	*limited export*

This fresh, uncured cheese, delectably rich and creamy, is made from the whey, or milky liquid, that is drained from the curd in making Provolone, Mozzarella, or other cheeses. Lighter and smoother then whipped Cottage Cheese, not at all salty, with a mild flavor verging on sweetness. Up to 10% whole milk is added to American-made Ricotta, making it richer and creamier.

Ricotta is an important ingredient in many Italian dishes such as *lasagne, manicotti, canelloni.* It is also used in cheese cakes and other desserts. Dry Ricotta is pressed and sliceable like Farmer's or Cream Cheese. Dry or moist Ricotta is very perishable. It should be snowy white; yellowing indicates that it is too old.

In Italy, Ricotta is sometimes dried and used for grating or crumbled into salads. As a fresh Pot Cheese, it can be topped with fresh or preserved fruit and is very good with black coffee. Mixed with Gorgonzola it makes a savory spread and appetizer for dry white wines such as Pinot Bianco, Orvieto, or Trebbiano.

RICOTTA PECORINO (also Ricotta Salata)

Not to be confused with fresh Ricotta, these are young, briefly cured, sheep's milk cheeses, similar to unaged PECORINO ROMANO. Mild but distinctive sheep flavors make it delicious as a snack cheese.

ROBIOLA

ORIGIN	*Piedmont/cow's, sheep's, or goat's milk*
TYPE	*fresh or soft-ripened/45–50% fat*
TASTE	*mild and creamy to pungent*
APPEARANCE	*small discs, sometimes boxed; creamy white to yellowish interior*
AVAILABILITY	*limited export*

A family of mostly fresh, creamy cheeses produced mainly in the Piedmont and Lombardy from the milk of goats, sheep, or cows, sometimes in combination. All are soft-ripened and range from the mild *Annabella* made from cow's milk to the strong-smelling *Robiola Introbio*.

Robiola Alba, from cow's milk, is fragile with creamy, salty flavors and a fresh, soft consistency. *Robiola di Roccaverano* is made of sheep's and goat's milk and has a drier, chalkier texture and a pleasant tang. *Formaggio del Bek* shows a mountain goat on the label although goat's milk is mixed with cow's milk and/or sheep's milk to make it. It is sold in a small soft mound that is very delicate when fresh but becomes saltier as it loses moisture. *Robiola Introbio* is a washed-rind cheese with a more assertive aroma. At perfect ripeness, it is luscious and creamy, with a faint aroma of truffles hovering about it. It can quickly become slimy and strong-smelling, with the "dirty socks" smell associated with French *Pont l'Evêque* or very ripe American *Liederkranz.* Considered an exceptional cheese when perfectly ripe.

The leading dairies that produce Robiola cheeses are Osella, Mauri, and Carmagnola in the Piedmont and Lombardy.

ROMANO *see* Pecorino Romano

SAN BERNARDO DOLCE

This cheese comes in small, crusty mounds shaped rather like fat, homemade biscuits. It has a semi-soft, slightly elastic, ivory interior that becomes creamier and more assertive in flavor, but never really ripens. San Bernardo *piccante* is drier and does ripen, becoming saltier and more pungent with age. The *dolce* is good with light red wines such as the Cabernets and Merlots of Trentino; the stronger *piccante*, however, demands sturdier reds.

SCAMORZE

ORIGIN *Latium/buffalo's milk*
TYPE *pasta filata/44% fat*
TASTE *mild, slightly salty*
APPEARANCE *sold in white or yellowish apple-sized ovals, sometimes with a loop on top*
AVAILABILITY *general export*

Originally made in the Abruzzi exclusively of buffalo milk, this plastic-curd cheese is now more common to the hills around Rome. Basically it is dried Mozzarella, the best still from milk of the water buffalo, although much of it is now made from cow's milk. Mild and chewy, it is saltier than Mozzarella and sometimes lightly smoked, which gives it an appealing mushroom flavor reminiscent of a damp forest. Expensive but highly prized by Italian cheese connoisseurs, it becomes dried out when it is too old. Scamorze, fresh or smoked, is often sliced and covered with fresh Tuscan virgin or other fine olive oil.

STRACCHINO

ORIGIN *Lombardy/cow's milk*
TYPE *fresh/50% fat*
TASTE *mild and delicate*
APPEARANCE *white and smooth interior; rindless; sold in slabs or loaves*
AVAILABILITY *limited export*

Stracchino cheeses have a delicate, lactic flavor similar to American Cream Cheese but milder and somewhat more acidic. Usually ripened quickly—within two weeks—they tend to become drier, stronger, and more flavorful with age, but should not exhibit the bitter or metallic flavors that affect some cheeses.

The name comes from *stracca,* which means "tired," and refers to the condition of the cows as they made their way to winter pastures after summer grazing. This does not apply anymore, if it ever in fact did. Stracchino is sometimes mixed with herbs or other flavorings. Stracchino CRESCENZA is the richest, creamiest Stracchino.

TALEGGIO (also Taleggio di Monte)

ORIGIN	*Lombardy/cow's milk*
TYPE	*semi-soft/48% fat*
TASTE	*mild and piquant to quite pungent, depending on age*
APPEARANCE	*flattish cylinders with clear paraffin covering, thin surface mold, straw-yellow interior, semi-soft*
AVAILABILITY	*general export*

Sometimes erroneously classified as one of Lombardy's *Stracchino* cheeses along with Gorgonzola, Taleggio actually has a family of its own. It is similar to the monastery cheeses because of its soft, smooth paste of pale yellow that darkens as the cheese ripens. Most factory Taleggio is bland and semi-soft, with a faintly acidic, mildly piquant finish that begins to sharpen within a few weeks. Taleggio di Monte, ripened in the caves of the Valsassina, matures quickly and becomes runny and quite pungent in aroma and flavor to the point of overripeness, a state which some cheese fanciers adore. *Formagelle d'Artavaggio* and *Tortalpina* are considered Taleggio relatives.

Taleggio is a fine after-dinner cheese with balanced red wines like Carema, Gattinara, or Valpolicella.

TOMA DI CARMAGNOLA

A regional cheese of the Piedmont, semi-soft in texture with mild, somewhat salty flavors. Quite lovely when fresh, but very little is exported.

TOMINO DEL MONFERRATO

A cow's milk cheese from the Piedmont with a mild, lactic flavor and pliant, semi-soft texture, Tomino del Monferrato is bland and pleasant, but not especially interesting. Although it is an old cheese, it has only recently begun to be exported.

TORTALPINA

Flat, pancake-like cylinders of soft-ripened, washed-rind cheese of the Taleggio family. Rich and creamy but not sharp, Tortalpina is quite luscious when not overripe. It should be slightly springy and full inside its rind, not sticky or overly runny. Export is limited, and it is available only at specialty cheese shops.

TORTAS

This is a fairly new genre of cheeses that have recently become very popular, though some consider them rather gimmicky. *Torta* means "cake" in Italian and these cake-like cheese loaves are composed of alternating layers of fresh cheeses and various flavorings of fruits, nuts, herbs, and the like. The basic *torta* mix is a combination of MASCARPONE, ROBIOLA, and sometimes fresh butter.

Torta con basilico is made of DOLCELATTE GORGONZOLA alternating with layers of basil and pine nuts. It is one of the best of the *tortas.* Others are composed of the basic *torta* mixture and alternate layers of such things as figs and bitter almonds, Scotch salmon, white truffles, walnuts, and green olives. Extravagant and luxuriant cheese treats, they are—not surprisingly—very expensive.

VALFIORE

Valfiore is Italy's closest approximation to Brie. A soft-ripened cheese with a thin, velvety white rind, it is creamy like Brie when fully ripe, with a mild, buttery flavor. Very limited export.

VECCHIO MULINO

Vecchio Mulino comes in a flattish cylinder with a bloomy white rind and is made in the Piedmont from cow's milk. Young versions have creamy, yellow paste and delectable, lightly salty flavors. The cheese gets stronger, and sometimes bitter, with age; it is best when young, clean, and fresh.

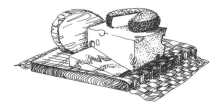

◆◆◆

GERMANY

Cheesemaking appears to have been underway in Germany over 1,000 years ago, mostly in the northern regions around the Baltic port cities of Hamburg and Bremen. The oldest style of German cheeses are the fresh *Sauermilchkäsen*—sour-milk fresh cheeses—that need no rennet. Still an important part of domestic production, these cheeses are rarely exported because they are so perishable.

In the Middle Ages, cheesemaking was fostered in the monasteries. By the fourteenth century the use of rennet made a wider variety of cheeses possible. In 1730 Frederick II of Prussia tried to encourage German cheese production by setting up a model farm with Dutch instructors, promising rewards to those who learned to make cheese from them. It worked—but resulted in the fact that most German cheeses have foreign origins: Limburger (Belgium), Emmentaler (Switzerland), Bavarian Blues (France and Italy), and others.

About 75% of German cheeses are produced today in Bavaria, where the mountain meadows of breathtaking Tyrol support a flourishing dairy industry. But cheese is also produced in other districts and the three principal ones are these: (1) The Northern Plain, stretching inland from the Baltic to just south of Hanover and Braunschweig. Most of the sour-curd cheeses, such as Handkäse, come from the area around these cities. (2) The Central Highlands, including the Rhineland and upper Bavaria. Sour-curd cheeses are produced around Frankfurt, German versions of Camembert and Brie and Edam around Nuremberg. (3) The Allgäuer Alps, in southwestern Germany near the Bodensee and the Swiss-Austrian border. Germany's best and most familiar cheeses come from here.

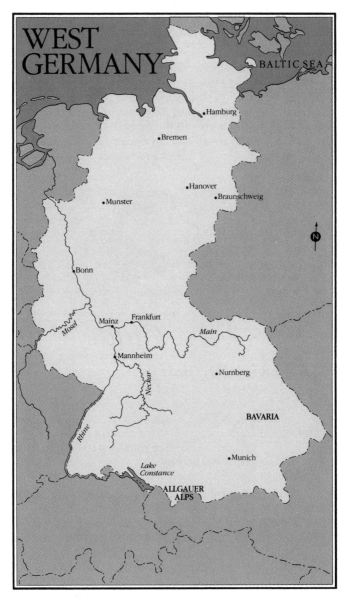

Although the potent-smelling Limburger and Romadur, Tilsit and, perhaps to *cognoscenti,* the Hand Cheeses, may seem most typical of the German style and preference, there is lately tremendous interest in the milder cheeses such as the Swiss-like Emmentalers from Bavaria, Münster, Brie and Camembert, and the Butter Cheeses (Butterkäsen). Smoked cheeses such as Bruder Basil and flavored cheeses are also enormously popular. Processed cheeses flavored with everything from mushrooms to bacon to herbs and spices account for nearly half of the German cheeses exported to the United States. One of Germany's best groups of cheeses are the blues from Bavaria, marketed under such names as Bavarian Blue or Blue Bayou. Inspired mainly by the blues of France, they are higher in butterfat and creamier in texture, full and flavorful but less sharp and pungent than their prototypes.

In Germany, as in Scandinavia, cheese is very popular for breakfast, particularly the mild *Butterkäsen*. If you find yourself in Munich, pay a visit to the fabulous food emporium, Dallmayr's, where you will see an opulent array of gourmet food items and over 150 different cheeses.

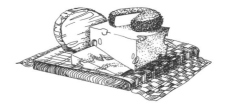

◆
Cheese Guide

ALLGÄUER EMMENTHALER

ORIGIN	*Allgäu/cow's milk*
TYPE	*Swiss/48% fat*
TASTE	*Swiss-like, perhaps milder*
APPEARANCE	*light yellow interior with large eyes; dark yellow to brownish rind on wheels from 22 to over 200 pounds*
AVAILABILITY	*general export*

Made in the traditional style of true Swiss, though milder in flavor, Allgäuer Emmenthaler is one of Germany's best cheeses. Emmenthalers for export are made from pasteurized milk, but in Germany one can find *Bergkäse* or *Alpkäse* (mountain cheese) that is more like Swiss Gruyère and made exclusively from raw milk. Made in the High Alps of the southern Allgäu, Bergkäse is rarely, if ever, exported. It may contain up to 60% butterfat, and it is well worth looking for in Germany.

Allgäuer Emmenthaler has the same uses as other Swiss-type cheeses—as an after-dinner cheese, for snacks or sandwiches, and accompanied by beer or medium-bodied reds.

BAVARIAN BLUE

ORIGIN	*Bavaria/cow's milk*
TYPE	*blue vein/70% fat*
TASTE	*rich, creamy, zesty*

APPEARANCE *white or ivory interior with blue veins or mottling; white bloomy rind*
AVAILABILITY *general export*

An excellent creamy blue so high in butterfat (70 percent) that it is almost a triple cream. This is one of Germany's newer cheeses, developed in the last several years as a combination bloomy-rind (soft-ripened) and blue mold cheese. It is soft, creamy, and mellow in taste with the sourish tang of blue mold. It is not as sharp as EDELPILZ, which has a more robust flavor and a crumbly texture. Though quite popular, Bavarian Blue does not have the highly individual character of the classic blues such as Stilton and Roquefort, which makes it a good choice for people who find those cheeses overpowering.

Bavarian Blue is very spreadable, excellent with fresh fruit, on French bread or neutral crackers, and with smooth, well-aged red wines.

BIANCO

A mild-tasting, cream-enriched, semi-firm loaf cheese of the TILSIT family. It is 55% butterfat and its pale yellow interior has numerous small holes.

BIAROM *see also* Caramkäse

A semi-soft cheese similar to Danish ESROM and sometimes called German Port Salut. Made in Bavaria, it comes in foil-wrapped loaves, plain or variously flavored with peppercorns, onion, paprika or caraway.

BIERKÄSE *see* Limburger and Weisslacker

Bierkäse means "beer cheese." It has been widely copied in the United States wherever there is a considerable German population and is similar to American BRICK.

BLUE BAYOU

A German blue cheese sold in cylinders. Only 60 percent butterfat, it is not as rich as Bavarian Blue and is more sliceable than spreadable. It is an agreeable cheese but lacks the definition of character and flavor found in other blues.

BRUDER BASIL *see* Caramkäse

BUTTERKÄSE (also Damenkäse)

ORIGIN *West Germany/cow's milk*
TYPE *semi-soft/50% fat*
TASTE *mild, buttery*
APPEARANCE *pale yellow, smooth interior, sold in loaves or sausage shapes*
AVAILABILITY *general export*

The generic group known as Butter Cheeses are very popular

in Germany, where they are often called *Damenkäsen,* or "ladies' cheeses," because of their exceeding mildness. They are soft-textured and bland, with the consistency of sweet butter; the best are without holes of any sort. Their widest use is as a breakfast or sandwich cheese, or for snacks.

CAMEMBERT

ORIGIN	*Bavaria/cow's milk*
TYPE	*soft-ripened/45–50% fat*
TASTE	*creamy, faintly piquant or sour*
APPEARANCE	*creamy off-white interior with soft white rind*
AVAILABILITY	*general export*

The attempt at French-style Camembert doesn't quite hit the mark, though it can be fairly flavorful and appealing at perfect ripeness. Even then, however, it tends toward bitterness. Try to buy it as fresh as possible. Germany also produces canned Camembert, which has a peculiarly cloying taste that bears little resemblance to genuine Camembert and is downright unpleasant when too old or ripe.

CARAMKÄSE

ORIGIN	*Bavaria/cow's milk*
TYPE	*monastery/45–60% fat*
TASTE	*mild, sometimes smoked*
APPEARANCE	*pale yellow, interior with semi-firm texture and few holes; smoked versions have brown rind*
AVAILABILITY	*general export*

A popular bland cheese. Smoked versions are more aromatic and piquant in flavor, with a pronounced smokiness. *Bruder Basil* and *Biarom* are the best-known export brands. Bruder Basil is often flavored with caraway seeds or other spices.

EDAM

German version of the Dutch EDAM but paler and milder, with a more pliant texture.

EDELPILZ (also German Blue)

ORIGIN	*Bavaria/cow's milk*
TYPE	*blue vein/45% fat*
TASTE	*rich, creamy, with pronounced moldy character*
APPEARANCE	*chalk-white mottled with blue pockets*
AVAILABILITY	*general export*

A fine blue cheese of crumbly texture and assertive piquant flavors, Edelpilz is very rich but not sharp or overly salty. It is not as creamy as BAVARIAN BLUE but is an excellent after-dinner cheese, eaten with full-bodied Saint-Emilion or a sturdy Rhône like Hermitage.

FRISCHKÄSE

ORIGIN *Germany/cow's milk*
TYPE *fresh/45–85% fat but some as low as 1%*
TASTE *fresh and tangy like cottage cheese*
APPEARANCE *loose white curds*
AVAILABILITY *general export*

This category includes a variety of fresh curd cheeses known by names such as *Zieger, Klatschkäse, Topfen, Luckeleskäse.* There are also several varieties made without rennet from soured milk and a lactic starter: *Buttermilchquark* is made from buttermilk; *Speisequark* from partially skimmed milk; *Rahmfrischkäse* is Speisequark enriched with cream; *Schicht-käse* has several layers of curd cheeses, one of skimmed curd alternating with another of full-fat curd. These cheeses are often served at breakfast or luncheon with fruit, raw vegetables, and spicy condiments.

GAISKÄSLE

ORIGIN *Allgäu/cow's and goat's milk*
TYPE *goat/50% fat*
TASTE *red rind: strong and aromatic; white rind: milder*
APPEARANCE *flat discs of yellow paste interiors with reddish-brown or white rind*
AVAILABILITY *domestic only*

The red-rind version is similar to ROMADUR. Ripe within two to three weeks of making, it is pungent and smelly with a yellow, smooth paste. The white-rind variety is dipped in a solution of whey-Camembert culture to encourage the growth of its fleecy rind. It ripens in 11 days and is milder, with the moldy hint of mushroomy flavors. Both versions are made from raw goat's milk mixed with 20–40% pasteurized cow's milk. As they mature, they take on more of the sharpness of goat cheeses.

HANDKÄSE (also Hand Cheese)

ORIGIN *Harz Mountains, Mainz/cow's milk*
TYPE *strong-smelling/10% fat or less*
TASTE *pungent*
APPEARANCE *various sizes and shapes, though usually round; hand-formed and irregular, soft*
AVAILABILITY *general export*

This is one of Germany's oldest cheeses made mostly from

skimmed sour milk. Its name, meaning "hand cheese," refers to the fact that the farmhouse variety is shaped by hand into flat discs, cylinders, or other shapes. Like all SAUERMILCHKÄSEN, even its mildest forms seem strong in flavor and odor to the uninitiated; some are startlingly pungent and overpowering, particularly at room temperature. Nevertheless Handkäse has its ardent adherents, who like it as a snack with raw onions, oil and vinegar dressing, and beer or cider. The Germans sometimes use it to flavor their beer, dropping in little bits of cheese that melt in the liquid.

Pennsylvania farmers of German descent made the first American Hand Cheese, and it is now also made in the Midwestern United States.

HOPFENKÄSE

ORIGIN	*Westphalia/cow's milk*
TYPE	*semi-soft/40% fat*
TASTE	*spicy, pronounced zest of hops*
APPEARANCE	*small, rindless, hand-molded spheres*
AVAILABILITY	*limited export*

Hopfenkäse is similar to another hop-flavored cheese called *Nieheimer*—both are made without rennet, using sour milk and heating it before collecting the curd. Caraway seeds may be added to Hopfenkäse; salt, caraway, and sometimes beer or milk are mixed into Nieheimer after five to eight days of ripening. The cheeses are dried and packed in casks between layers of hops, which give the cheese its zesty flavor and aroma. Farmhouse versions often become hard enough to use for grating; factory-made cheeses are usually softer and sometimes flavored with cumin. They are best, of course, with a good lager beer such as Pilsener Urquell.

LIMBURGER

ORIGIN	*Allgäu/cow's milk*
TYPE	*soft-ripened, strong-smelling/20–50% fat*
TASTE	*strong, spicy, piquant, even gamy at times*
APPEARANCE	*smooth yellow paste, with yellow, brown, or reddish rind in rectangles or large blocks*
AVAILABILITY	*general export*

The king of the smelly cheeses, Limburger actually originated in Belgium around Liège, but today most of it is made in Germany. As with all strong-smelling cheese, the taste for Limburger is an acquired one, but some people adore it. Like its cousin ROMADUR, Limburger is a surface-ripened cheese with a washed rind. It spends three months in a humid atmosphere acquiring its pungent aroma and soft texture. The export cheeses are often much riper by the time they reach their destination and can be devastating to the nostrils of the unprepared. Copies of these cheeses are now made in America and are especially popular in the northern Midwest.

Germans enjoy Limburgers mostly with beer. There is, in fact, a sub-type of Limburger called *Bierkäse* (Beer Cheese). Bierkase is aged five to six months and is firmer than Limburger; some say it tastes like bacon. There is another Limburger known as *Frühstückäse* or "breakfast cheese," which is barely ripened and slightly milder. Limburgers go with pretzels, dark breads, raw onions, radishes, and the like.

MÜNSTER

ORIGIN	*Germany/cow's milk*
TYPE	*monastery/45–50% fat*
TASTE	*mild to pungent*
APPEARANCE	*smooth, pale yellow paste, few holes; thin reddish-yellow skin*
AVAILABILITY	*general export*

As with most European Münsters, German versions are generally more flavorful than American, especially when fully ripened. German Münster is not quite so highly flavored as the original cheese from Alsace, but it has a distinctive, often powerful aroma. Its texture is semi-soft and smooth. Young Münsters are milder, but robust red wines suit either type.

NIEHEIMER *see* Hopfenkäse

ROMADUR

ORIGIN	*Bavaria/cow's milk*
TYPE	*monastery, surface-ripened/46% fat*
TASTE	*strong*
APPEARANCE	*white, semi-soft interior, few holes; smooth, honey-brown or reddish rind, sold in small foil-wrapped bars*
AVAILABILITY	*general export*

Germany's cross between American LIEDERKRANZ and its own Limburger, Romadur is a creamy, surface-ripened cheese cured more briefly than Limburger—three to four weeks. Young Romadur is mild, plump, and resilient and ripens within a few weeks to the point of runniness. It is assertive and smelly, but not as strong as Limburger. Romadur that is too old is very runny and sticky, or hard and dried out.

Romadur is good with dark beer or ale, pumpernickel bread, and green onions and olives. Spicy, dry Gewurztraminer is a good wine choice.

SAUERMILCHKÄSE

ORIGIN	*Harz Mountains, Mainz/cow's milk*
TYPE	*strong-smelling/10% fat or less*
TASTE	*pungent flavors and aroma*
APPEARANCE	*generally small, sold in various shapes (discs, bars, spheres, etc.)*
AVAILABILITY	*limited export*

The sour curd cheeses are widely popular in Germany. Powerful in flavor and aroma, they are based on *Sauermilch-quark,* a sort of cottage cheese made without rennet or starter. They are low in fat (10% or less), high in protein, and specialized in taste—sharp, piquant, even rank. They are also very pronounced in aroma. Two of the best-known varieties are *Harz* and *Mainz,* named for the areas where they are made. Other varieties are named for shape or method of production: *Stangen* (bar), HANDKÄSE (hand-molded), *Korb* (basket), *Spitz* (pointed), *Kochkäse* (cooked cheese). Some are flavored with spices such as caraway or cumin.

In Germany they are most often eaten as a snack and accompanied by beer or cider.

TILSIT (also Tilsiter)

ORIGIN	*Germany/cow's milk*
TYPE	*monastery/30–50% fat*
TASTE	*full-bodied, pungent*
APPEARANCE	*ivory to yellow semi-soft interior; dark yellow rind, sometimes rindless*
AVAILABILITY	*general export*

German Tilsit is another of those "accidental" cheeses. It was first made in East Prussia by Dutch farmers who were trying to make Gouda. A Dutch farmwife cured her cheese in too damp a cellar, so the story goes, and it became soft and sharp and developed cracks instead of the smooth, mild, and firm interior of Gouda. East Prussia is now a part of the Soviet Union, but Tilsit is made all over Germany, in both factories and farmhouses.

Farmhouse Tilsit, made from raw milk, is ripened for about five months and is by far the strongest version. Factory Tilsit is made from pasteurized milk and aged a shorter time and is therefore milder. But it is still rather pronounced in flavor and even more so in aroma, falling between a Danish Port Salut and a mild Limburger. Its numerous cracks are its hallmark, as is its slightly sourish aftertaste.

Germans like it with Spätlese whites from the Rhinepfalz, but sturdy reds can also accompany it.

WEINKÄSE

Named "wine cheese," these are mild, round, usually soft cheeses whose creamy smoothness makes them good with the lighter Rhine and Moselle wines.

WEISSLACKER (also Weisslacker Bierkäse)

ORIGIN *Bavaria/cow's milk*
TYPE *surface-ripened/3% fat*
TASTE *mild to pungent, depending on age*
APPEARANCE *thin, whitish, glossy rind; smooth, semi-soft, white interior, few holes; sold in 2- to 3-pound squares*
AVAILABILITY *limited export*

A popular cheese with Bavarian-style beer, Weisslacker (the name means "white rind") ranges from mild and moist as a young cheese, to pungent and strong-smelling when more mature. As it ages it becomes not unlike Limburger. The stronger ones, aged up to five months or more, are often called *Bierkäse* (beer cheese). Securely wrapped in plastic film and refrigerated, unaged Weisslacker keeps from two to four weeks, depending on how strong you like it. Bierkäse will keep considerably longer.

Both cheeses go best with dark breads, sausages, onions, and beer or ale.

ZIEGER

ORIGIN *Germany/cow's milk*
TYPE *whey/under 10% fat*
TASTE *fresh, mild*
APPEARANCE *white, curdless mass*
AVAILABILITY *domestic only*

Originally Zieger was the name for Sauermilchquark in the Allgäu, but today it is properly used to describe a fresh whey cheese that resembles Ricotta.

◆◆◆

HOLLAND

heese, much more than windmills, the Zuider Zee, or even Hans Brinker and his silver skates, is practically synonymous with Holland. Holland's yellow wheels of Gouda and red balls of Edam are the most well-known and widely exported cheeses in the world. The country's broad, flat expanses of rich pasturage, many below sea level, easily accommodate the large herds of sleek, velvet-coated, black-and-white Friesian cows native to northern Holland. Of the more than 600 million pounds of cheese produced annually, 450 million pounds are exported to over 100 countries.

Earliest records of cheese-making in Holland go back at least 800 years but the process probably was well underway before that. Cheese molds from the fourth century have been found and the court of the emperor Charlemagne enjoyed the fruits of the labors of dairymen from Friesland. By the Middle Ages the Dutch were important exporters, first by land and then by sea, to the far corners of Europe. As Holland's commercial empire grew, so did the importance of their two most dependable, long-keeping cheeses: Gouda (which the Dutch pronounce "howdah") and Edam. By the early seventeenth century they were being exported to the Americas. Because they lasted so well, they were good sailors' cheeses. Edam even came in handy in a sea battle in 1847, when the Uruguayan fleet, under U.S. command, defeated an Argentine fleet by using the well-ripened spheres as cannonballs!

Cheese-making began on private farms in Holland—there are still individual farmers who produce their own Gouda—but by the Middle Ages, cheese cooperatives began to appear and weekly cheese markets brought producers together to vend their wares. One of the oldest such markets is that of Alkmaar, in northwest Holland. Farmers transported their cheeses by barge to this medieval port town. There they were placed on wooden "cheese sleds" with red or green painted runners, brought to the central square, and laid out in neat, rectangular piles. Cheese producers still come to the Alkmaar cheese market each week from April through September to haggle over prices of various lots of cheese.

Edam and Gouda, Holland's two most famous cheeses, are very similar in taste and consistency, but Edam is firmer. It is the only cheese in the world, in fact, that can hold a perfectly spherical shape, largely because of its lower fat content. Traditionally, cows were milked twice daily on Dutch farms. The evening milk was kept overnight, skimmed the next morning, and mixed with the fresh, whole morning milk. From this mixture Edam was made. As a result, the smooth mellow cheese was firm enough to be formed into round balls, the shape in which it was cured and aged. Gouda, from southern Holland, was traditionally made twice a day from fresh whole milk. Higher in butterfat, it has a softer, creamier consistency than Edam, and is sometimes lighter in color. Both cheeses are popular in *broodjes,* delectable little sandwiches sold in *broodjewinkels,* Dutch sandwich shops. They can be found all over Amsterdam and feature sausages, roast meats, cheeses, hot little rolls with good Dutch butter, and beer—"fast food" Dutch-style.

Spice-flavored cheeses such as Leyden and certain varieties from Friesland, are less well-known than Gouda and Edam, both of which have been widely imitated throughout the world.

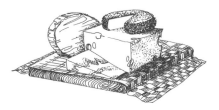

◆
Cheese Guide

EDAM

ORIGIN	*northern Holland/cow's milk*
TYPE	*semi-firm/40% fat*
TASTE	*smooth, mellow, sharper with age*
APPEARANCE	*grapefruit-sized spheres coated in red or yellow wax; ivory to pale gold interior with few holes*
AVAILABILITY	*general export*

Edam differs from Gouda in that it is made from partially skimmed rather than whole milk. It is less creamy in texture and the paste firms up quicker, allowing it to be molded into distinctive spheres. Originally its natural rind was rubbed with vermilion-dyed cloth. Today Edams produced for export are coated with red paraffin; in Holland, a yellow coating is more common.

Unlike Gouda, all Edam is factory-produced today. It is Holland's second most important cheese, after Gouda, and accounts for 16% of all cheese produced. Regular Edams generally weigh about four pounds. Baby Edams vary in weight from a pound and a half to just under two pounds. Edams in loaf shapes, weighing from five to eight pounds, are also available. Young Edam is mellow but savory; when too young it can be sourish. Mature Edam, aged up to a year, is drier, stronger and saltier. Its keeping qualities were demonstrated in 1956 when a tin of Edam was found by members of an expedition to the South Pole. The cheese was sharp but edible. It had been left there by the Scott expediton of 1912, 44 years earlier.

Edam is sometimes spiced with cumin, which adds an extra touch of flavor. It is a fine snack or luncheon cheese, easy to slice or dice for sandwiches and salads, and tastes best with dark beer or light-bodied red wines.

FRIESE NAGELKAAS (also Friesian or Friesian Clove)

ORIGIN	*Friesland/cow's milk*
TYPE	*semi-soft/20–40% fat*
TASTE	*tangy, spicy, but fairly mild*
APPEARANCE	*cartwheels weighing up to 20 pounds with brown-yellow rim*
AVAILABILITY	*general export*

The aroma of clove is quite pronounced in Nagelkaas—the name comes, in fact, from the Dutch word *nagel,* or "nail," which the little club-headed clove resembles. Friesian cheeses are sometimes spiced with both clove and cumin, sometimes with one or the other. Skimmed-milk Friesians are harder than those made from whole milk. Fresh buttermilk is sometimes used with whole milk to add tang.

The best are aged about six months. Although a dry Gewurztraminer can perhaps handle them, Nagelkaas are too spicy for most wines, and work best with beer or ale.

GOUDA

ORIGIN	*southern Holland, Utrecht/cow's milk*
TYPE	*semi-soft/48% fat*
TASTE	*mild, buttery*
APPEARANCE	*cartwheels of various sizes with yellow (sometimes red) waxed rind; yellow interior with few small eyes*
AVAILABILITY	*general export*

Mild and versatile Gouda owes its appealing texture to the double heating of the curd in the whey before draining off the liquid completely. Young or current-aged Gouda, on the market within a few weeks of making, is the mildest. Aged Gouda, particularly that aged a year or more, is firmer in texture and more developed in character and flavor.

Gouda is made in both factory and farmhouse. The farmhouse product is superior, especially for aging, as it is usually made from whole raw milk. Both whole and skimmed pasteurized milk are used in factory Gouda. Genuine farmhouse Gouda is marked *Boerenkaas* ("farmer cheese") on the rind, but little is exported. Particularly fine Boerenkaas is made in the Stowijk area near Utrecht.

Factory Gouda is a dependable bland cheese, but mature farmhouse Gouda is a true delicacy. Aged a year or longer, it develops sweet but full cheddar-like flavor without ever losing its smoothness. It turns a rich gold color and is saltier than young Gouda. Although the natural rind toughens considerably with age, the inner texture remains buttery and somewhat flaky. Some experts can identify the region, and sometimes the town, where an aged Gouda originated.

Gouda is sold plain or sometimes spiced with cumin or other spices (one popular version is known as Pompadour). Its versatility as a snack or table cheese gives it a variety of uses. It is good with pickles or jam, goes with almost any wine or beer, and is widely used in recipes. The Dutch make *kaasdoop* with it, a sort of fondue served with potatoes and dark bread.

KERNHEM

ORIGIN	*Holland/cow's milk*
TYPE	*double cream, monastery/60% fat*
TASTE	*full, rich, creamy*
APPEARANCE	*flat disc with red rind*
AVAILABILITY	*domestic*

This cheese came about by accident, back in the days when Edam was made in the farmhouse. Sometimes a young, ripening Edam would collapse into a smelly disc. Though it was no longer Edam it tasted good, with rich flavors and a soft, creamy consistency. About 20 years ago, the Netherlands Institute for Dairy Research developed a way to make the cheese intentionally. Today though perhaps more potently flavored, it is comparable to traditional monastery-type cheeses such as French St. Paulin. Mature in four weeks, Kernhem makes a good after-dinner cheese but needs a full-bodied red wine to accompany it.

LEYDEN (also Leiden)

ORIGIN	*Leyden/cow's milk*
TYPE	*semi-soft/20–40% fat*
TASTE	*mellow, with spicy tang*

APPEARANCE	*light yellow interior speckled with caraway and/or cumin; natural rind cylinders*
AVAILABILITY	*general export*

One of the most venerable of spiced cheeses, Leyden (known in Holland as *Komijne kaas*) is peppered with seeds of caraway and cumin. Spiced cheeses from other countries are derived from the Leyden concept—Norwegian Nokkelost is a copy of it. Spiced layers of curd are sandwiched between two unspiced layers; the curds are then pressed together and ripened. Leyden is made both on farms and in factories. Farmhouse Leyden, made from partially skimmed milk plus buttermilk, is marked with two keys, symbol of the city of Leyden.

Leyden makes a flavorful sandwich cheese or snack. The Dutch often eat it with *jenever,* the juniper-flavored drink that evolved into gin. Stalwart reds such as Zinfandel can handle it, too.

MAASDAMMER

A Swiss-type cheese modeled after Norwegian JARLSBERG, with medium to large eyes and mellow, nutty flavor, Maasdammer is not as well-defined as its prototype. The name comes from the River Maas, which bisects Holland and empties into the North Sea at Rotterdam. The best-known export brand is *Leerdammer.*

MON CHOU

ORIGIN	*Holland/cow's milk*
TYPE	*double cream/73% fat*
TASTE	*rich, creamy, faintly tart*
APPEARANCE	*soft, white, rindless and foil-wrapped discs*
AVAILABILITY	*domestic only*

A very rich double cream (almost a triple cream) with a delicious, faintly sourish tang, Mon Chou was developed very recently in Holland and has not yet been exported.

ROOMKAAS

ORIGIN	*Holland/cow's milk*
TYPE	*semi-soft/60% fat*
TASTE	*bland and buttery*
APPEARANCE	*wheels weighing 11 pounds with waxed rinds; pale yellow, smooth interior*
AVAILABILITY	*general export*

Roomkaas means "cream cheese" and refers to the fact that this cheese is cream-enriched. Its smooth, sliceable texture and mild creamy flavors make it popular in Holland for sandwiches and as an appetizer with cocktails. Light, fruity red or white wines suit it very well also.

SCANDINAVIA

he Scandinavians are the world's great cheese adaptors—most of the cheeses of Denmark, Sweden, Norway, and Finland are modeled after cheeses from other countries. The practice began during World War I, when imports from France, Holland, Switzerland, and Germany were interrupted. Ever lovers of good cheese, the Scandinavians were forced to develop their own cheese industry. This they proceeded to do extremely well, particularly in Denmark. Today some of the world's most popular and widely enjoyed cheeses are Scandinavian adaptations: the famous blues of Denmark, Jarlsberg of Norway, Danish Port Salut (Esrom), Samsoe, and Havarti.

Cheese-making in Scandinavia actually dates to the days of the Vikings. It was necessary in those rugged northern lands to set aside food for the long, dark winter. Cheese-making was a way of preserving the plentiful spring and summer milk for use in leaner times. Cheese by-products were also a basic part of the Viking diet. They ate curds and buttermilk and one of the earliest Viking drinks, referred to in the Sagas, was *skyr,* or curdled milk.

However, little evidence remains of the cheese-making of Viking days. It was the Cistercian Monks of the Middle Ages who fostered the first real interest in cheese. Since meat was forbidden them, they ate quantities of cheese instead and learned to substitute an extract of Venus Flytrap for animal rennet to separate the curd from the whey. This bizarre curdling agent must have done its work well. To this day, the Danes are particularly fond of the soft-ripening monastery-type cheeses, and they prefer cow's milk to goat or sheep cheeses—both inclinations inherited from the early monks. Cheese production, however, remained localized and

SCANDINAVIA

LAPLAND

Kiruna

FINLAND

SWEDEN

NORWAY

Bergen

Oslo

Helsinki

Stockholm

North Sea

Goteborg

Gotland

Aalborg

Aarhus

Copenhagen

DENMARK

Baltic Sea

restricted in scope until the nineteenth century. Even then, expansion of the industry was hampered by the limited amount of grazing land in Scandinavia. Only 3% of Norway and 10% of Finland are arable. Denmark is the exception—95% of its land is available for cultivation. The dairy industry thrives in northern Denmark and she is among the five largest exporters of cheese and butter in the world.

Denmark, like the other Scandinavian countries, produces its own versions of Brie, Cheddar, Swiss, Camembert, Fontina, and many other cheeses. But the Danish government, anxious to give certain cheeses their own identity, has recently succeeded in having Danish names adopted for many cheeses. Swiss-style Danish Emmentaler, for instance, still exists, but a whole range of similar cheeses—each with subtle variations in character—now carry the name of the town of origin plus the suffix -*bo:* Danbo, Fynbo, Tybo, Elbo, and so on.

Most of the Scandinavian imitations tend to be somewhat blander than the original and are sometimes thought of as lacking in character. They are, however, of consistent quality and relatively inexpensive, which explains why they are so popular in worldwide markets. Norwegian Jarlsberg is currently the single most popular Scandinavian cheese.

Although few are exported, indigenous cheeses are still available in Scandinavia. Goat cheeses may be found in the mountains; reindeer cheese is still made in Lapland, fresh sheep's milk cheese in Iceland. Scandinavia is also a huge producer and exporter of processed and flavored cheeses.

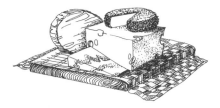

♦

Cheese Guide

AMBROSIA

ORIGIN	*Sweden/cow's milk*
TYPE	*monastery/45% fat*
TASTE	*mild, buttery, faintly tart*
APPEARANCE	*pale yellow, semi-soft interior with scattered irregular holes; sold in thick wheels 10–12 inches in diameter*
AVAILABILITY	*general export*

One of Sweden's most popular exports, Ambrosia is a mild, semi-soft cheese similar to German Tilsit or French Port Salut though not as strong in flavor or odor. It makes a good snacking or sandwich cheese, slices easily, and keeps reasonably well. Because it is generally sold young, after ripening for about two months, it lacks character as an after-dinner cheese.

BLUE CASTELLO (also Blå Castello)

ORIGIN	*Denmark/cow's milk*
TYPE	*blue vein/double cream/70% fat*
TASTE	*creamy, rich, tangy accent*
APPEARANCE	*soft, white interior with strips or splotches of blue mold; sold in small blue and white paper boxes*
AVAILABILITY	*general export*

This soft, creamy blue cheese is one of the most popular Scandinavian cheeses. Its base is cow's milk enriched with cream and its spreadable consistency makes it very popular as a cocktail cheese on crackers or rounds of firm pumpernickel. The cheese is innoculated with both white and blue molds and ripened for as long as three weeks, during which time it develops a bloomy rind. When young it is mild with a piquant accent from the blue mold. As it ages, the edible rind becomes reddish-brown, and the cheese develops a stronger flavor and aroma. The young version is good with crisp, dry white wines like Sauvignon Blanc, Pinot Blanc, and Sancerre; the more mature cheese can handle a light Rhône red.

CREMA DANIA (also Crema Danica)

ORIGIN	*Denmark/cow's milk*
TYPE	*double cream/72% fat*
TASTE	*mild, richly creamy*
APPEARANCE	*creamy ivory interior with bloomy white rind; sold in 6-ounce rectangular boxes*
AVAILABILITY	*general export*

A queen among double creams, Crema Dania is so rich that it is almost a triple cream (minimum 75% fat). Mild, very clean in taste, and well known for its even ripening, it is similar to Brie and Camembert but has a less distinctive flavor. Crema Dania was developed by Danish cheese-maker Henrik Tholstrup in imitation of the soft, creamy texture and subtle flavors of Brie.

Suitable as an after-dinner cheese, Crema Dania is best served on French bread with smooth, well-matured Bordeaux reds, California Cabernets, or Pinot Noirs.

CREME ROYALE

A Danish double cream very like CREMA DANIA but sold in foil-wrapped cubes.

DANABLU (also Danish Blue)

ORIGIN	*Denmark/cow's milk*
TYPE	*blue vein/50% fat*
TASTE	*richer than most blues, but less piquant*
APPEARANCE	*white to ivory paste with deep blue veins; sold in 4-inch deep cylinders or rectangles*
AVAILABILITY	*general export*

Danish Blue was developed just before World War I by a farmer named Marius Boel, who baked special loaves of barley bread to get the mold for his cheese. Modeled after Roquefort which is made from ewe's rather than cow's milk, Danablu is higher in butterfat and therefore richer in taste. Though not as piquant or salty as Roquefort, nor as complex, it has vivid, zesty flavors that make it one of the most popular of the blue veins. Its semi-soft texture slices and spreads easily, but it also crumbles nicely for use in salads. Although its flavors sharpen with age, it can be mixed with sweet butter to cut the salty edge. Excellent with dark bread and crudités or fresh fruit, Danablu needs a full-bodied red wine to stand up to it.

DANBO

ORIGIN	*Denmark/cow's milk*
TYPE	*semi-firm/45% fat*
TASTE	*bland, buttery*
APPEARANCE	*light yellow interior with holes and yellow or red wax rind*
AVAILABILITY	*general export*

This is one of the Swiss-style, SAMSOE family of cheeses for which Denmark is famous. It has the mild, nutty, and faintly sweet flavors common to the numerous Swiss imitators. It is sometimes spiced with caraway seeds and marketed as King Christian IX. There is also a low-fat Danbo containing only 20% butterfat.

DANISH CHEF

A brand of processed cheeses from Denmark containing various flavorings of herbs, salmon, and other piquancies.

ELBO

One of the mildest of the Danish SAMSOE cheeses, Elbo's bland, buttery flavors and Swiss-like texture make it an ideal sandwich cheese for children's lunchboxes. Sold in loaf shapes.

ESROM (also Danish Port Salut)

ORIGIN	*Denmark/cow's milk*
TYPE	*monastery/45–60% fat*
TASTE	*mild when young, strong and earthy when mature*
APPEARANCE	*ivory to yellow interior with irregular holes; thin, yellow to tan rind; often foil-wrapped*
AVAILABILITY	*general export*

Esrom, from the town of the same name, is often likened to French PORT SALUT, but its flavors are more pungent and its aromas—especially with age—are very pronounced, making it actually closer to German TILSIT. Current-aged Esroms are milder, but, because it is a surface-ripened cheese and continues to age within its thin, washed rind, exports tend to be strong. It is sold in large blocks or loaves and is sometimes flavored with caraway, peppercorns, or herbs.

Esrom is best accompanied by dark beer or full-bodied red wines.

FONTINA (also Fontal)

ORIGIN   *Denmark, Sweden/cow's milk*
TYPE   *Swiss/45–50% fat*
TASTE   *bland and buttery to faintly tangy to strong*
APPEARANCE   *pale yellow interior with few holes; rind covered in red or yellow paraffin*
AVAILABILITY   *general export*

Modeled after the Italian FONTINA D'AOSTA, Scandinavian Fontina is softer and more pliable in texture but tends to be fuller-flavored. The Danish version in particular is somewhat sharper than the subtler and more complex Italian original. The Scandinavian Fontinas are very popular as snack or sandwich cheeses.

FYNBO

One of the sharper cheeses of the Danish SAMSOE family, Fynbo originated on the island of Fyn. In texture it resembles young Gouda. The thick, natural rind allows it to keep well for weeks if securely wrapped and refrigerated.

GAMMELOST

ORIGIN   *Norway/cow's milk*
TYPE   *blue vein/5% fat*
TASTE   *sharp, aromatic, strong mold character*
APPEARANCE   *yellowish-brown interior; sold in tall cylinders with brownish rind*
AVAILABILITY   *limited export*

This is one of the oldest Scandinavian cheeses. *Gammel* means "old"; *ost* means "cheese." The cheese itself is not old, but it is prepared in the traditional way from sour, instead of fresh, milk. It is both surface-ripened and has blue-green internal mold. During ripening it is stored on straw soaked with the juice of juniper berries. As it matures—four to six weeks in modern factories—furry tufts of mold cover the exterior and are worked by hand into the cheese. It is very low in butterfat—four or five percent—but nonetheless strong-smelling due to the mold. Grammelost is definitely an acquired taste but is quite popular in Norway. It is occasionally available in export markets around Christmas.

GJETOST (also Getost, Ekte Gjetost)

ORIGIN   *Norway, Sweden/goat's and cow's milk*
TYPE   *whey/10–33% fat*
TASTE   *buttery rich, faintly sweet and caramel-like*
APPEARANCE   *brown paste sold in small, foil-wrapped rectangles*
AVAILABILITY   *general export*

This is one of the most original Scandinavian cheeses, and also one of the oldest. Life was hard in earlier days and nothing was wasted if it was edible. Originally Gjetost was made from the whey of goat's milk. It was cooked till the sugars caramelized and it became a brown paste that was eaten on bread like butter. Today it is generally made from the whey of both goat's and cow's milk. When made from goat's milk alone, it is called Ekte Gjetost and is quite strong. The whey is heated slowly to evaporate the water, and lactose and brown sugar are sometimes added.

It is excellent as a breakfast cheese with strong, black coffee, but is generally considered an acquired taste because of its overtones of sweetness and consistency resembling peanut butter. It is best sliced thin with a cheese plane.

Swedish Getost is a goat cheese that may or may not be made from the whey. Norwegian Mysost is made in the same way as Gjetost, but entirely from cow's milk.

GRADDOST

ORIGIN *Sweden/cow's milk*
TYPE *semi-soft/60% fat*
TASTE *mild buttery*
APPEARANCE *pale yellow interior with small, irregular holes; yellow or red paraffin-covered rind; sold in cylinders or blocks*
AVAILABILITY *general export*

A popular butter cheese (*graddost* means "butter cheese"), it is mild in taste, but rich enough to be a double cream. Graddost slices easily for sandwiches and is good with fresh fruit. Beer and light, dry wines suit it well.

HAVARTI

ORIGIN *Denmark/cow's milk*
TYPE *semi-soft, monastery/45-60% fat*
TASTE *full-flavored with piquant finish*
APPEARANCE *pale yellow interior with numerous irregular holes; sold in blocks or loaves, often foil-wrapped*
AVAILABILITY *general export*

Originally known as Danish Tilsit, this distinctive cheese was developed by Mrs. Hanne Nielsen on her experimental farm called Havarti. It has a mild but piquant flavor and is semi-soft in texture after ripening for two to three months. As it ages it gets stronger in flavor and can become quite pungent. Low-fat Havartis are made but are available only in Denmark; the double cream versions have 60% butterfat and are more acid in taste. Light fruity reds go best with young Havarti, sturdier ones with the more mature cheeses.

HERRGARDSOST

ORIGIN *Sweden/cow's milk*
TYPE *Swiss/45% fat*
TASTE *rich, nutty, mellow*

APPEARANCE *ivory to yellow interior with round holes;*
yellow paraffin rind
AVAILABILITY *general export*

Sweden's version of Swiss Emmentaler is consistently good but milder and less flavorful than the prototype. It is matured three to eight months. In Sweden a full-cream version is known as *Herrgard Elite.*

Herrgardsost is very popular in Sweden. A version called *Drabant* is a mild and popular breakfast cheese. A genuine and well-made Herrgardsost "weeps" when allowed to mature 12 months or more—the eyes become moist and glossy and the flavors well-developed. It enjoys all the uses of a good Swiss: as a snack, sandwich, or mild after-dinner cheese with light red wines.

JARLSBERG

ORIGIN *Norway/cow's milk*
TYPE *Swiss/45% fat*
TASTE *mild, delicate, faintly sweet*
APPEARANCE *rich yellow with large eyes; yellow wax*
rind; sold in large wheels
AVAILABILITY *general export*

The Norwegians firmly deny that Jarlsberg is a copy of Swiss Emmentaler, which it strongly resembles in both appearance and flavor. It is more delicate and buttery, however, and doesn't have the nutty aftertaste associated with genuine Emmenthaler. It is also sweeter. Jarlsberg's enormous popularity has some cheese specialists wondering if all the milk needed to produce it can possibly come from Norway alone. Generally reliable in quality, Jarlsberg keeps well for weeks.

Dry white wines and fruity reds partner it best and it goes with a wide assortment of foods and snacks.

KUMINOST *see* Nökkelost

LAPPERNAS RENOST (also Lapland)

ORIGIN *Swedish Lapland/reindeer milk*
TYPE *reindeer/high fat*
TASTE *strong*
APPEARANCE *unique dumbbell shape*
AVAILABILITY *local only*

Made from the high-fat milk of reindeer, Lappernas Renost is the world's most northerly cheese The milk is so rich that it has very little whey; consequently the cheese has a naturally low moisture content. It is strong-flavored and so hard that the Lapps sometimes break off chunks and dunk them in their coffee. Since reindeer give less than 30 quarts of milk per year, the cheese is rare and seldom gets far from Lapland.

LAPPI

Finland's pale ivory, Swiss-style cheese, very firm in texture.

MARIBO

ORIGIN *Denmark/cow's milk*
TYPE *semi-soft/45% fat*
TASTE *mild to strong, depending on age*
APPEARANCE *yellow interior with many small irregular holes; sold in wheels or cylinders*
AVAILABILITY *general export*

Maribo is similar to, but not as strong as, Danish Port Salut, even though the riper versions are fairly pronounced in aroma and flavor. The Danes prefer the stronger Maribo, which is aged six to ten months and is firmer in texture than the commonly exported younger cheese. Maribo is sometimes flavored with caraway seeds and labeled King Christian IX (Caraway-flavored DANBO is also called King Christian IX).

MOLBO

The Danish version of Dutch EDAM, Molbo has a similar flavor and is quite good.

MYCELLA

ORIGIN *Denmark/cow's milk*
TYPE *blue vein/50% fat*
TASTE *mildly tangy*
APPEARANCE *rindless blocks or cylinders, white interior with greenish veining*
AVAILABILITY *general export*

This Danish blue is modeled after Italian Gorgonzola. It gets its name from the *mycelium* mold that is used instead of the bread mold common for other blues, including Danablu. The veins are more greenish than blue and the flavor is milder than Danablu. It is often exported in foil-wrapped wedges.

NÖKKELOST (also Kuminost)

ORIGIN *Norway/cow's milk*
TYPE *semi-firm, spiced/20–40% fat*
TASTE *spicy*
APPEARANCE *smooth yellow interior dotted with seeds; natural- or waxed-rind cylinders or blocks*
AVAILABILITY *general export*

Nökkelost is the Norwegian copy of LEYDEN, the spiced cheese of Holland. Flavored with caraway, cumin, and clove, the basic cheese is semi-firm, mild, and somewhat oily like Leyden. Some are made from skimmed milk and are therefore lower in fat.

Nökkelost is versatile as a snack or sandwich cheese and is also used in cooking, where it lends its spicy flavors to quiche and other dishes. In Norway it is often served with beer or a shot of Aquavit.

PORT SALUT, DANISH *see* Esrom

SAGA BLUE

ORIGIN	*Denmark/cow's milk*
TYPE	*blue vein, double cream/60% fat*
TASTE	*creamy, piquant*
APPEARANCE	*small cylinder with white bloomy rind; soft ivory interior with light veining*
AVAILABILITY	*general export*

Saga Blue is a Danish Brie with blue mold, the only such combination existing to date. The delicate veining gives it a mildly piquant tang, but it is extremely rich and sometimes almost a triple cream with 70% fat. Fruity, lightly sweet wines go well with it, such as Riesling or Chenin Blanc.

SAMSOE

ORIGIN	*Denmark/cow's milk*
TYPE	*Swiss/45% fat*
TASTE	*Swiss-like, but milder*
APPEARANCE	*yellow interior with cherry-sized holes; yellow rind*
AVAILABILITY	*general export*

This is the Danish national cheese, well-loved by the Danes for its mild, nutty character. Named for the island of Samsoe where it was developed, this cheese has spawned a number of the "-bo" cheeses that are similar in taste and texture but vary in shape and size; among them ELBO, FYNBO and TYBO.

All of the Samsoe cheeses lend themselves to a variety of uses because of their mild yet distinctive character. Mellow red wines are their best companions, but beer or ale goes well, too.

SVECIAOST (also Svecia)

ORIGIN	*Sweden/cow's milk*
TYPE	*semi-soft/30–60% fat*
TASTE	*bland, buttery*
APPEARANCE	*pale yellow interior with irregular small holes*
AVAILABILITY	*general export*

Sweden's version of Dutch GOUDA is typically mild and bland with a smooth, semi-soft texture. Aged for 12 months, it takes on more pronounced flavors and aromas and develops a distinctive character of its own. Most of what is produced, however, is quite young. Sometimes it is spiced with caraway and/or cumin.

TYBO

A loaf-style cheese of the SAMSOE family.

SWITZERLAND

My earliest memory of Switzerland is of waking up on a frosty morning in a cosy billow of down to the sound of tinkling cowbells. Despite the chill, and the fact that I couldn't find my slippers, I was irresistibly drawn to the window just in time to see a line of dairy cows pass in single file below and head up the grassy incline toward the alpine meadows.

Cooking instructor and author Michael Field once wrote that Switzerland has "an almost mystical reverence for cows." Switzerland is so mountainous that there is very little arable land in this small country—and what exists is mostly covered in vineyards. Aside from the Alps themselves, Switzerland's greatest "natural resource" are cattle. They provide the endless supply of rich milk to produce her famous cheeses. Cheese-making is a proud local and communal affair in Switzerland. The lives of whole families revolve around the cow. In summer entire households move with their small dairy herds to the mountains so that the cows can graze with bovine abandon on the succulent grasses of the high meadows. The Alps are dotted with little wooden buildings known as *sennhütten* (cheese huts) that serve as alpine dairies.

The return to the valleys in autumn is often marked with festival and celebration. In the Oberland near Bern, the herders announce the descent of the herd from their lofty summer pastures by rolling blazing logs down the mountainside. The cows, festooned with garlands of wildflowers and with milking stools tied to their harnesses, are led down to winter in the valleys.

The best-known Swiss cheeses—Emmentaler and Gruyère —keep well over long periods of time, a quality important in

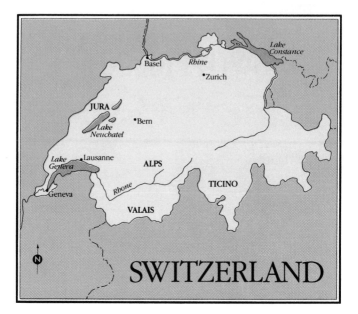

a mountainous country where transportation is slow. Emmentaler, the "holey" cheese that is imitated the world over, has such good keeping quality that traditionally a single wheel of Swiss is given to a child at birth, to be eaten at christening, wedding and funeral! Another wheel might be buried with the dead to nourish them on their journey.

There are over 100 varieties of cheese produced in Switzerland, but most of them are available only locally. The dozen or so that are exported, however, generate a steady worldwide demand because of the high quality of genuine Swiss cheese. Although Swiss cheese has many imitators, none can quite match its special flavors, the effect of the unique climate and grasslands on the cows' milk. Swiss chocolate benefits from these conditions as well.

Sbrinz, Appenzeller, Raclette, Tête de Moine, Vacherin Mont d'Or—these and the other cheeses of Switzerland are produced in more than 1500 small dairies, each headed and supervised by a Master Cheesemaker under the regulation and strict controls of the Switzerland Cheese Association. Swiss regulations prescribe in detail the diet for dairy cows and absolutely prohibit the use of additives or coloring agents. The Swiss also make their own versions of several foreign cheese varieties, including Brie, Camembert, Limberger, Münster, various goat cheeses, and others.

All Swiss cheeses are labeled *Switzerland* on the rind. "Imported" Swiss does not necessarily mean you are getting Switzerland Swiss. It could be Finnish, Austrian, Swedish, or American, and although these cheeses can be quite good, they are not the same as genuine Swiss. Some of the worst

"Swiss" is the pre-sliced and packaged variety. Cheese without any natural eyes at all is sometimes stencilled to provide it with "Swiss" holes!

◆

Cheese Guide

ALPKÄSE (also Bergkäse)

ORIGIN *high Alps/cow's milk, some goat's milk*
TYPE *Swiss/45% fat*
TASTE *2 types, similar to Emmentaler: large wheels stronger in flavor*
APPEARANCE *wheels of various sizes, 2 to 50 pounds*
AVAILABILITY *local only*

The term Alpkäse, which literally means "cheese made in the Alps," includes a wide variety of firm to semi-soft cheeses sometimes made from a mixture of cow's and goat's milk. Its flavors, particularly when made from whole or skimmed cow's milk, are similar to Emmentaler's—slightly sweet, nutty, and mellow. Large wheels of twelve to fifty pounds are generally stronger in flavor and sold under such names as *Hasliberger, Bündner, Justistaler, Piora;* smaller rounds of two to five pounds, such as *Mutschli, Tummeli,* and *Bratkäsli,* are softer in texture and aged for shorter periods.

Both are used as table cheeses, snacks, for melting, or in salads. In Switzerland, try with the red wine known as Dole.

APPENZELLER

ORIGIN *All Switzerland, particularly Appenzell/cow's milk*
TYPE *Swiss/45% fat*
TASTE *mild to very fruity and faintly spicy*
APPEARANCE *pale gold interior with small, sparsely scattered holes; sold in small cartwheels with convex sides; smooth brownish rind*
AVAILABILITY *general export*

Appenzell, also the name of a Swiss *canton,* or province, means "alpine cell" and refers to the mountain valleys occupied by families of dairy-herders in summer. Appenzeller is similar to both Emmentaler (Switzerland Swiss) and Gruyère but has a higher moisture content than either. It is much more highly flavored than Emmentaler and even tangier than Gruyère. That is because after it is made, Appenzeller is cured by washing it in a mixture of cider, white wine, and spices for four or five days. This adds an extra fillip of flavor that makes it a popular choice for fondue.

Appenzeller Räss, made from partially skimmed milk, is bathed for several weeks in the mixture and is therefore quite pungent, spicy, and sharp (*räss* means "sharp"). It is mostly available only in Switzerland.

Whole-milk Appenzeller goes well with fresh fruits, nuts, light red and white wines; it is fine for spicing up fondues or cheese sauces. Rässkäse calls for more full-bodied red wines.

BELLELAY (also Tête de Moine)

ORIGIN	*Bern/cow's milk*
TYPE	*semi-firm/45–50% fat*
TASTE	*rich, spicy, salty*
APPEARANCE	*sold in cylinders 5 inches high; pale gold, smooth-textured interior; brownish rind*
AVAILABILITY	*limited export*

Originally produced in the Monastery of Bellaye in the Jura of Bern, Tête de Moine is a fall and winter specialty—made only from the rich milk of summer when the cows feed on fresh grass. Its name means "monk's head" and comes from the fact that a horizontal cut through the cylinder reveals a pale center surrounded by a darker ring and brownish rind that looks somewhat like the tonsured head of a monk.

A pressed cheese of firm texture, Tête de Moine is rich but subtly flavored and delicately spicy. It is an excellent dessert cheese, often served on crusty bread sprinkled with pepper. Serve it with crisp, dry white wines or full-bodied, fruity reds.

EMMENTALER

ORIGIN	*chiefly Bern/cow's milk*
TYPE	*Swiss/45% fat*
TASTE	*mellow, lightly rich, nutty*
APPEARANCE	*light yellow-gold with cherry-sized holes and natural rind; large wheels (up to 220 pounds) with convex sides; Switzerland is stamped concentrically over face of rind*
AVAILABILITY	*general export*

Fifty-five percent of Switzerland's cheese production is Emmentaler, the original Swiss cheese. Of that 55%, more than 70% is exported worldwide. It is Switzerland's oldest cheese; one of its ancestors was probably the *caseus Helveticus* (cheese from Helvetia, or Switzerland) known in classical Rome. Although its production and distribution have been considerably modernized since farmhouse days, when it was made by alpine herdsmen called *sennen,* it is still made chiefly in small dairies and exclusively of raw milk.

Emmentaler is referred to as a "cooked" cheese because the curds are first separated from and then heated in the whey. It is ripened in three stages: first in a cool cellar where it is bathed in brine; then in a warm cellar where fermenting bacteria are added; then in a cool, humid room for five to ten months. The cheese gets its cherry-sized holes, or "eyes," from the gases that expand inside during fermentation.

When buying Emmentaler, make sure that there are not too many holes and that the rind is not unnaturally swollen.

An expert can tell when a cheese is of good quality simply by tapping the whole cheese and listening to it. A good sign of ripe Swiss is "weeping eyes,"—that is, the glistening of salt and butterfat in the holes.

The mildly rich, nutty flavors of Emmentaler make it delightful for a variety of uses—snacks, luncheon sandwiches, or after dinner with fruit and nuts. It is the basic cheese for Swiss fondue (often used in combination with Gruyère or Appenzeller) and is often grated as a condiment.

Many countries make versions of this cheese, including the United States, Finland, Austria, Australia, Argentina, Germany, Denmark, and Ireland, but none can match the sweet, distinctively nutty flavor of the original.

GRUYÈRE

ORIGIN	*Fribourg, Jura Alps/cow's milk*
TYPE	*Swiss/45–50% fat*
TASTE	*fruitier and sometimes saltier than Emmentaler, sweeter than French Gruyère*
APPEARANCE	*yellow-amber interior, with pea-sized holes spaced well apart; brownish wrinkled rind; sold in wheels at around 100 pounds*
AVAILABILITY	*general export*

Swiss Gruyère, named for its village of origin in the canton of Fribourg, is moister than Emmentaler and more highly flavored. It has a similar sweet nuttiness about it but is stronger because of longer aging, usually for ten to twelve months. It is also sold after six months, but is considered to be too old if it is sandy in texture or if cracks have developed in the brownish rind. As with Emmentaler, weeping eyes are a sign of maturity and quality.

It is an excellent choice for fondue, but is also a fine after-dinner cheese with, perhaps, a mature Cabernet Sauvignon.

RACLETTE

ORIGIN	*Valais/cow's milk*
TYPE	*Swiss/50% fat*
TASTE	*mild, nutty, mellow*
APPEARANCE	*yellow to amber interior with small scattered holes; brown rind; sold in wheels*
AVAILABILITY	*general export*

Raclette is made in all parts of Switzerland for local consumption but the Raclettes of the Valais are the best and most famous. Similar to Gruyère, it was originally used as a melting cheese in the dish it is named for. The word *racler* means "to scrape." The dish known as *raclette* is made by cutting the wheel of cheese in half and exposing it to an open fire. The melted cheese then is scraped onto a plate and served with boiled potatoes, gherkins, and pickled onions. It is a delectable dish, but Raclette is equally enjoyable in slices or as a soup topping or in sauces.

Raclette

Making successful raclette is a matter of getting the right cheese. Dealers may try to sell you Appenzeller, Royalp, or Gruyère, but such cheeses are not for raclette. Only the cheese called "Raclette" has the correct combination of fat and moisture, producing a tasty, broiled specialty. Originally, raclette was made by cutting the wheel of cheese in half, exposing the cut surface to an open fire, and scraping off the melted cheese. This romantic method is not always convenient, since guests have to eat the servings one-at-a-time before the broiled cheese cools. Modern chefs prefer to slice the cheese, setting the slices under the broiler. Accompanied by black bread, boiled potatoes, pickled vegetables, and white wine, raclette makes a quick, delicious meal.

ROYALP (also Swiss Tilsit)

ORIGIN	*eastern Switzerland/cow's milk*
TYPE	*monastery/15–50% fat*
TASTE	*mild, fruity*
APPEARANCE	*pale yellow interior with firm smooth texture and small holes; ochre rind; sold in small wheels*
AVAILABILITY	*general export*

Similar to German TILSIT, Royalp is milder and not as strong smelling. It is one of Switzerland's newer cheeses, developed near the turn of the century. Made from whole or skimmed milk, its medium-firm texture and fullish, piquant flavors make it a good snack or after-dinner cheese, as well as a tasty garnish for salads. It is good with beer or dry rosé and dark bread.

SAANEN

ORIGIN	*Berne/cow's milk*
TYPE	*Grana/45–50% fat*
TASTE	*similar to Sbrinz when mature, milder when young*
APPEARANCE	*smooth, hard, yellow interior; sold in thick cylinders or wheels weighing 40–90 pounds*

Saanen is very similar to Sbrinz, though harder and less subtly flavored, and is used primarily for grating. Sometimes aged as many as seven years, it is one of the hardest and most durable of cheeses. In the canton of Berne where it originated, it was the custom to make and dedicate a wheel of

Saanen for each newborn. At every birthday thereafter, a piece of it was eaten until the entire cheese was consumed.

As an appetizer, it is sometimes served in thin slivers shaved off with a cheese plane; it is good with crisp, dry white wines such as Fendant or Neuchatel.

SAINT OTHO

ORIGIN *all Switzerland/cow's milk*
TYPE *Swiss/under 10% fat*
TASTE *mild*
APPEARANCE *ivory to pale yellow interior with small holes; orange rind; sold in small wheels*
AVAILABILITY *general export*

One of the best of the low-fat cheeses that are widely produced in Switzerland, Saint Otho is also one of the few exported. The fat content averages about 4%, as against 25–50% for most cheeses. Its mild flavor and soft texture make it a useful sandwich and snack cheese, especially for those on low-fat diets. Cheeselovers, however, may find it rather boring.

SAPSAGO

ORIGIN *Glarus/cow's milk, skimmed*
TYPE *hard, Grana/under 10% fat*
TASTE *sharp, pungent, herby*
APPEARANCE *hard, greenish interior shaped into 4-inch cones*
AVAILABILITY *general export*

Sapsago, also known as *Schabzieger* in Switzerland, is a hard cheese made entirely from skimmed milk. Its unusual herb flavor and greenish color come from a specially-grown variety of clover that is added to the cheese to give it pungent flavor. It is used almost exclusively as a grating cheese because of its hard, dry consistency. It keeps indefinitely and makes a useful garnish for salads or a piquant condiment for spreads and dips.

SBRINZ (also Spalen)

ORIGIN *Central Mountains/cow's milk*
TYPE *Grana/45–50% fat*
TASTE *very rich and mellow*
APPEARANCE *dark yellow interior; yellowish-brown rind; sold in flat cylinders*
AVAILABILITY *general export*

Sbrinz is principally a grating cheese. However, because of its smooth rich flavors, flaky texture, and mellow, lingering aftertaste, it can, like Italian Grana Padano, stand on its own. During World War II, in fact, when the Italians could not get Parmesan or Grana, they used Sbrinz. It is one of the oldest of Swiss cheeses and probably the one mentioned by Pliny. It is aged for two to three years and can be excellent with bold reds such as Barbera or Zinfandel.

A younger version, aged up to a year and a half, is known as Spalen and is used more as a table cheese, but also for flavoring in casseroles or pasta. It is also served as an appetizer with wine or cocktails.

TÊTE DE MOINE *see* Bellelaye

VACHERIN FRIBOURGEOIS

ORIGIN	*Fribourg/cow's milk*
TYPE	*monastery/45–50% fat*
TASTE	*mild, sometimes sourish and resiny*
APPEARANCE	*pale yellow interior of semi-firm texture; sold in wheels of 12 to 18 pounds*
AVAILABILITY	*limited export*

This mountain cheese, considered a great delicacy by some cheese connoisseurs, has more a pronounced flavor than Gruyère, of which it is thought to be a predecessor. A specialty of the canton of Fribourg, it is often used to make strong fondues. It is also a fine after-dinner cheese with balanced reds from Pomerol or the Médoc. Fribourgeois is not easily found outside of Switzerland, but specialty cheese shops have it on occasion.

VACHERIN MONT D'OR

ORIGIN	*Swiss Jura/cow's milk*
TYPE	*monastery, soft/45% fat*
TASTE	*rich, creamy, subtle*
APPEARANCE	*flat 1-pound cylinders with thin beige crusty rind, pale creamy interior*
AVAILABILITY	*fall and winter, limited export*

This delectable mountain specialty, highly prized by cheese connoisseurs, is more widely available than Vacherin Fribourgeois but only at certain times of year. A seasonal cheese, it is made from whole cow's milk taken in the last four months of the year. The rind is repeatedly washed with white wine, which results in a stiff, smooth beige crust. When fully ripe, Vacherin has a soft, creamy smoothness, runny enough to be eaten with a spoon. Its flavor has a delicate savor and fresh, appealing aftertaste, sometimes with slightly piney or resinous aromas from being wrapped in sprigs of spruce or balsam.

Its creaminess and subtle complex character make it greatly sought after in late fall and winter. It is delicious with fruity white wines such as Swiss Fendant and Rieslings from California or Germany, but it is equally fine with mature Bordeaux from the Médoc.

◆◆◆

OTHER EUROPEAN COUNTRIES

everal other European countries produce notable cheeses, some of which are ancient and famed. Greek Feta, widely imitated, is one of the world's oldest, probably a descendant of the ewe's milk cheese made by Polyphemus the Cyclops in Homer's *Odyssey.* The Greeks eat enormous quantities of cheese, some 33 pounds per capita annually. Kefalotyri, Haloumi, and Kasseri are also important cheeses in Greece and Cyprus.

Two other old world cheeses are Rumanian Bryndza and Bulgarian Kashkaval, both made from ewe's milk. Similar to Bryndza is Hungarian Liptauer, a fresh cheese flavored with spices, chopped onions, and other savories. It is popular in much of central Europe and in great demand for export.

Austria's best known cheese is Mondseer, a soft, strong-smelling monastery cheese. Austria also makes creditable Swiss, Gruyère, and Tilsit-type cheeses modeled after their prototypes. Belgium's claim to fame in cheesedom stems from the fact that pungent and smelly Limburger originated there, on farms near Liege. Limburger is no longer made in Belgium, having long since become a specialty of Germany, and more recently, the United States. Belgium's reputation for rank, aggressively flavored cheeses is nobly upheld, however, by Hervé and Remoudou.

Spain and Portugal have strong local cheese-making traditions, but neither country has yet managed to produce a much-sought after export cheese. Best-known is Spanish Manchego, a savory sheep's milk cheese that is widely made but sporadically exported. Highly esteemed locally are Queso de Cabrales, a goats milk blue made in Asturias, and Queso de Serra from Portugal, a mountain cheese.

Cheese Guide

BRYNDZA (also Brinza)

ORIGIN *Rumania/ewe's milk*
TYPE *sheep/45% fat*
TASTE *tangy, rich, a bit sharp*
APPEARANCE *white and soft, or firm like chèvre*
AVAILABILITY *limited export*

Bryndza, made from sheep's milk, sometimes mixed with goat's milk, is one of the world's oldest cheeses, originating in central Europe, and made throughout regions of the Carpathian Mountains (Poland, Czechoslovakia, Rumania, and Transylvania). It is salty in taste, from being cured in brine, but rich and creamy, not overly sharp. It can be soft, moist and spreadable or semi-firm and drier, rather like Feta. In Hungary soft Bryndza is often used as the base for Liptauer-like spread or dip, flavored with herbs and spices.

FETA (also Telemes)

ORIGIN *Greece/sheep's or goat's milk*
TYPE *sheep or goat, soft//45–60% fat*
TASTE *rich, tangy, salty*
APPEARANCE *white, matured or stored in whey and brine bath*
AVAILABILITY *general export*

Although Feta is widely available, the Greeks themselves consume so much of it on a day-to-day basis that much of what we actually import is made in Italy. Some of the imported Feta is also made from skimmed or partially skimmed milk. In Greece, Feta from whole sheep's or goat's milk, which is very rich and creamy, is preferred. Although it is traditionally made from sheep's milk (Polyphemus's cheese was probably a Feta), modern factory-made versions incorporate goat or cow's milk. Feta is at its best aged four to six weeks. It should be purchased right out of its brine bath, where it stays moist and flavorful. (Feta is often referred to as a "pickled" cheese because it is cured and stored in brine.) As it matures it becomes sharper and saltier but will stay mild and moist longer if stored in milk.

Feta has been made for centuries in Greece and the Balkans, but the growing international taste for it means that it is now made all over the world. American, Australian, and Danish Feta are made from cow's milk and are very sharp in flavor. The Danish version is crumbly and may have a harsh taste. German and Bulgarian Feta are milder and creamier.

Feta is an excellent snack cheese and gives delightful bite and zest to salads. It melts quickly and is often used for cooking in such dishes as *stifado*, a cinnamon-flavored beef stew. Ouzo and Retsina are the recommended drinks in Greece, but dry Italian whites like Pinot Grigio or Orvieto also go well with it.

HALOUMI (also Haloumy or Halumi)

ORIGIN	*Greece, Cyprus/ewe's milk*
TYPE	*sheep/40% fat*
TASTE	*savory, salty, tangy*
APPEARANCE	*ivory color, firm consistency; kneaded and rolled, sometimes mixed with mint leaves, sold in loaves or blocks*
AVAILABILITY	*limited export*

Like Feta, Haloumi is cured in a brine solution and is therefore sometimes referred to as a "pickled" cheese. But Haloumi has a firmer, more pliable consistency, similar to the *pasta filata* of Italy, that comes from kneading and rolling the cheese while moistening it with warmed whey. Sometimes, in fact, it is quite stringy, and is generally creamier in color than chalk-white feta.

One of the best ways to eat it is the way they do on the island of Cyprus—it is cut into cubes or slices and sauteed in butter or grilled quickly over a fire. In a good Haloumi the savoriness is never sharp or biting, although it can be quite salty. The mint-flavored version (not often seen outside Greece) counters the saltiness and offers a fresh and unusual flavor of its own. Haloumi is also good in salads or melted on meat. The wines of Cyprus—red, white, or rosé—go well with it.

HERVÉ

ORIGIN	*Liège/cow's milk*
TYPE	*strong-smelling, monastery/45% fat*
TASTE	*pungent, tangy*
APPEARANCE	*soft, pale yellow cubes with reddish-brown outer rind*
AVAILABILITY	*general export*

This Limburger-like cheese—a member of the genre known as "stinking cheeses"—comes from the city of Hervé but its origins go back to the Middle Ages when it was made by monks in the monasteries of Liège. It comes in several different styles, including a low-fat version made from partially skimmed milk. Repeatedly drained of its whey, the cheese is cut in cubes, dipped in brine and matured in a damp room for three months. As it ripens, a reddish-brown bacteria develops on the surface, giving the cheese its pungent aroma and flavor. One of the best Hervé cheeses is REMOUDOU. Hervé is sometimes flavored with chives, thyme, parsley, or other herbs. It needs a robust wine or strongly hopped beer to offset its strong flavors.

KASSERI

ORIGIN	*Greece/sheep's or goat's milk*
TYPE	*sheep or goat, hard/40% fat*
TASTE	*salty, savory*
APPEARANCE	*white to pale gold with Cheddar-like consistency, natural rind; sold in large blocks*
AVAILABILITY	*general export*

Greek Kasseri is similar in appearance and taste to Feta, but is hard and often used, like Parmesan, as a grating cheese. It is sharp, salty, and savory, used a great deal in cooking, and, in fact, makes a delicious dish on its own called *saganaki:* slices of Kasseri are sauteed in a frying pan with a little butter. Very popular as an appetizer, the cheese is served sizzling hot with fresh lemon squeezed on it, and with pita bread.

An interesting American version of Kasseri is made in Wisconsin from cow's milk. It is pale gold in color and similar in texture to Cheddar, but sharper and saltier. It makes a good grating cheese and a snappy grilled cheese sandwich. Full-bodied red wines go well with it.

LIPTAUER (also Brinza or Bryndza)

ORIGIN	*Hungary/sheep's milk*
TYPE	*fresh/45% fat*
TASTE	*mild base, often flavored with spices, herbs, onions*
APPEARANCE	*basically white but commonly salmon-colored due to addition of paprika; sold in containers or small boxes*
AVAILABILITY	*general export*

Hungarian Liptauer originally came from Liptó, a section of northern Hungary that is now part of Slovakia across the Czech border. Traditionally, this fresh, white Pot Cheese, made mostly from sheep's milk with cow's milk occasionally mixed in, was stored in wooden barrels and scooped out with wooden ladles. Mixed with paprika, chopped onions, and butter and spread on crusty white bread or caraway rye, it makes a delicious afternoon snack with beer or wine. Often other flavorings are added, such as mustard, anchovies, beer, capers, even a dollop of caviar. In German-speaking countries it is this flavored mixture that is called Liptauer, while in Hungary it is the name for the basic Pot Cheese itself. Romanian BRYNDZA is similar.

The fruity white wines of Austria and Hungary suit it well and it is often served with *heurigen,* the fresh young wines of Austria that become available soon after harvest.

MANCHEGO

ORIGIN	*La Mancha, Spain/sheep's milk*
TYPE	*semi-firm/50–60% fat*
TASTE	*rich, mellow*

APPEARANCE   *light gold interior; low cylinders with dark or black rind*
AVAILABILITY   *general export*

Manchego is Spain's best-known cheese and was originally made from the sweet-scented milk of Manchego sheep that roamed the plains of La Mancha, the fabled birthplace of Don Quixote. Today it is widely made in several parts of Spain, in factories as well as by farmers. There are four stages of ripeness for Manchego: *fresco* (fresh), *curado* (aged three to thirteen weeks), *viejo* (aged over three months), and Manchego *en aceite* (cured up to a year in olive oil).

Manchego *curado* and *viejo* are the most widely exported; both are rich, flavorful, mellow cheeses. Some of them have up to 57% butterfat, making them practically double creams. Cheeses similar to Manchego are made in other parts of Spain and include *Grazalema* from Cadiz, *Oropesa* from Toledo or *Queso de los pedroches* from Cordoba.

Manchego is excellent with the full-bodied red wines of Spain—Rioja, Coronas, Cabernet Sauvignon, or Sangre de Toro.

MONDSEER

ORIGIN   *Austria/cow's milk*
TYPE   *monastery/50% fat*
TASTE   *full, pungent flavors*
APPEARANCE   *yellow, semi-soft interior with a reddish washed rind; sold in small wheels, sometimes boxed*
AVAILABILITY   *limited export*

Mondseer, from the Lake Mond area of Austria near Salzburg, is a type of MÜNSTER but much stronger in flavor and aroma than the Alsace or German versions. It could even be described as Limburger-ish, though its consistency is more like Münster. It is made from skimmed and whole milk and is sometimes known as *Mondseer Schachtelkäse* when sold in boxes.

Like most strong-smelling cheeses, Mondseer is good with beer or full-flavored red wines.

QUESO DE CABRALES

ORIGIN   *Asturias, Spain/sheep's and goat's milk*
TYPE   *sheep and goat, blue vein/50% fat*
TASTE   *sharp, piquant, and rich*
APPEARANCE   *low cylinder with crusty outer rind, crumbly blue-veined texture*
AVAILABILITY   *domestic only*

This cheese, considered a great delicacy, has the rich, sharp savor of combined goat's and sheep's milk, with some cow's milk added for smoothness. It is ripened for two to three months in limestone caves, where it develops blue mold and a flavor similar to Roquefort. Most of it is consumed in the region where it is made, but some may be found in the specialty food shops of Spanish cities, wrapped in leaves to retain its freshness and flavor.

QUESO DE SERRA

ORIGIN	*Portugal/ewe's milk*
TYPE	*sheep/40–50% fat*
TASTE	*creamy and mild to sharp and tangy*
APPEARANCE	*small cylinders or cakes, creamy whitish interior*
AVAILABILITY	*domestic only*

Queso de Serra is the mountain cheese of Portugal, widely produced but tremendously varied because it is still made by shepherds and farmers in remote regions. Some are made in low cylinders and ripened to a style and flavor similar to Manchego. Others are formed in small cakes or cylinders the size of Camembert and are similarly creamy and faintly piquant. The name means simply "mountain cheese" and it is often further distinguished by a regional name. *Serra da Estrella* is thought to be one of the finest types. Estrella has a creamy white paste and is eaten young, at two to three weeks. Aged longer, the cheese takes on a sharper, more pungent flavor. Extract of thistle flower is sometimes used as a curdling agent instead of animal rennet, although today rennet is commonly added. Thistle continues to be used, however, for the distinctive flavor and texture it gives the cheese.

Portuguese red wines, including the simple, everyday carafe wines, are excellent companions for these cheeses.

REMOUDOU

ORIGIN	*Battice, Liège/cow's milk*
TYPE	*strong-smelling, monastery/45–52% fat*
TASTE	*similar to Limburger*
APPEARANCE	*sold in small blocks or cubes of butter-colored, semi-firm paste, foil-wrapped and boxed*
AVAILABILITY	*general export*

One of the most distinctive of the HERVÉ cheeses, strong-smelling, even "stinky" when too ripe, although some prefer it this way. Its name means "after-milk," which is the milk taken from the cows just after lactation when it is richest in butterfat. It is sometimes referred to as a double cream, even though it is less than 60% fat. The history of Remoudou is preserved in a museum, converted from a former cheese factory in the town of Battice.

◆◆◆

USA & CANADA

ne way Americans reveal their diverse origins is through their love of cheese. The American taste for cheese has grown steadily since colonial days, when New Englanders tried to re-create the cheeses of their homeland. In trying to copy English Cheddars and Cheshires, early settlers in New York, Vermont, and elsewhere in New England, and eastern Canada set the stage for American imitations of Europe's famous originals— Emmentaler, Gorgonzola, Parmesan, Münster, Limburger, Roquefort, and others.

Some of these are very good, although they can scarcely be said to possess the distinctive—and mostly inimitable— character of their prototypes. The best New World cheeses, however—Canada's Black Diamond Cheddar, aged Sonoma Jack, Limburger, Canadian Oka, the Oregon and Iowa Blues, and a few others—deserve to be judged rather on their own merits than as imitations of something else. These are fine cheeses indeed. They are made by traditional methods, hand-tended and, though not widely available, are well worth seeking out.

Modern dairy technology in the United States has been something of a mixed blessing. While its vast production has made cheese widely available, it has at the same time fostered a taste for bland, characterless, packaged cheeses and pro-cessed varieties full of additives, emulsifiers, and artificial colorings and flavors. Subsequently, there has been a prolif-eration of imitation cheese products, some of which contain no dairy products whatsoever. These often find their way into partially pre-cooked "convenience" foods like frozen pizza and TV dinners.

America's technological prowess, however, has had its influence in the cheese world. As early as the mid-nineteenth century, production methods developed in the Herkimer County, New York, cheese factory were in demand in England, where American consultants helped the development of factory Cheddar. New York cheese-makers developed a successful, soft Cheddar relative called washed-curd cheese that could be ripened much faster than true Cheddar. And innovators in Wisconsin invented a stirred-curd cheese called Colby that was also distinctive and quick-ripening. Scientific research resulted in Canadian *Richelieu,* a monastery-type cheese similar to *Bel Paese.*

Two notable American originals are Brick, a Wisconsin-made, semi-soft, pungent cheese created in 1877, and Liederkranz, a creamy, soft-ripened cheese that becomes stronger as it matures. While Cheddar-style cheeses predominate in North America, there are also some excellent and distinctive blue-veins. The best are made in limited quantities and are available only in specialty cheese shops in the United States (Oregon Blue, Minnesota Blue) or by mail-order (Maytag Blue).

The Midwest—especially Wisconsin—is America's dairyland, but cheese is produced in at least 37 of the 50 states. Fortunately, growing interest in truly fine cheese has prompted new experiments. Word comes from Petaluma, California, of an excellent new goat cheese, and from Graham, Washington, of fine Cheddar and Brie. The West Coast has also come up with respectable versions of Brie and Camembert (Rouge et Noir brand) and the triple cream known as Rondele. Scattered pockets of local cheese production still exist across the United States and Canada. The burgeoning demand for good cheese from increasingly knowledgeable consumers should encourage further experimentation and, with luck, the birth of a great American original.

Cheese Guide

AMERICAN CHEESE

ORIGIN	*U.S.A./cow's milk*
TYPE	*semi-firm, Cheddar/fat content varies*
TASTE	*mild to sharp*
APPEARANCE	*varies*
AVAILABILITY	*domestic*

This umbrella term embraces all types of American Cheddar and Cheddar-style cheeses, but mostly it refers to the ubiquitous processed presliced sandwich cheese used in combination with ham, baloney, salami, or bacon and tomato. This along with other processed cheeses account for over half of American cheese consumption.

BLUES

ORIGIN	*U.S.A./cow's milk*
TYPE	*blue vein/50% fat*
TASTE	*varies from mild and creamy to salty and quite sharp*
APPEARANCE	*white with concentrated blue mold, usually crumbly-textured; mostly rindless; variously packaged*
AVAILABILITY	*domestic*

American Blue Cheeses from large manufacturers have the sharpness and crumbly texture sought for garnishing salads or use in cooking. As dinner or snack cheeses, however, they are less satisfactory and do not compare well to the best blues from France, Germany, and Denmark. Three specialty blues do, however, and are worth the special effort to find them.

OREGON BLUE:

Produced in Central Point, Oregon, this blue is soft-textured, very savory, and not too salty and has an excellent blue-mold character. It is mostly available on the West Coast.

MINNESOTA BLUE:

Made in Fanibault, Minnesota, this is another fine American blue, ripened in sandstone caves in southwestern Minnesota. Produced by the Treasure Cave Blue Cheese Company, it is available to a limited extent in the Midwest or directly from the company in Fanibault (55021).

MAYTAG BLUE:

This blue is made from the milk of a prize herd of Holstein-Friesian cows that graze on 1600 acres of rolling grasslands in Iowa. Superbly marbled and aged six months, Maytag Blue is chalk white, soft, and creamier in consistency than Oregon Blue. It is also tangier and saltier. It comes in two- or four-pound wheels or singly-packaged wedges, but is available only at a very few specialty shops or by mail from Maytag Dairy Farms, Rural Route 1, Box 806, Newton, Iowa 50208.

BRICK

ORIGIN	*Wisconsin/cow's milk*
TYPE	*semi-soft, monastery/50% fat*
TASTE	*faintly earthy to quite strong*
APPEARANCE	*pale yellowish, semi-soft interior, usually sold in rectangles or bricks*
AVAILABILITY	*domestic*

An American original, Brick was invented in Wisconsin in

1877 by John Jossi, an American of Swiss heritage. The cheese, which gets its name either from its shape or the fact that originally bricks were used to press out the whey and mold the curd, evolved from Mr. Jossi's production of Limburger. The basic procedure is the same but Brick cheese has less moisture than Limburger and is therefore firmer and more elastic.

When young, Brick is a mild, semi-soft cheese similar to other monastery-type cheeses such as French Saint Paulin. With age, however, it ripens into a very pungent cheese with a bitter rind. It is not quite as strong as Limburger and is best with dark breads, onions, and full-bodied beer or ale. Beer cheese is a variation similar to Brick and a descendant from the German Bierkäse. Beer cheese is popular in communities in the Midwest and the northeastern United States. The bitter rind on older beer cheeses should be removed before eating.

CHEDDAR, AMERICAN

ORIGIN	*U.S.A./cow's milk*
TYPE	*semi-firm, Cheddar/45–50% fat*
TASTE	*mild to sharp*
APPEARANCE	*ivory to orange interior, sold in cylinders, wheels or blocks; natural or waxed rinds*
AVAILABILITY	*general export*

Roughly 70% (over a billion pounds) of American cheese production are Cheddars. The first American Cheddar was produced in 1851 in Oneida County in upstate New York. New York Cheddar is still considered one of the best of American Cheddars.

Most American Cheddar is produced from pasteurized milk, but the best are still made from raw milk. (It is legal in the United States to use raw milk for cheeses aged over 60 days; the finest Cheddars are aged far longer.) The bitterness that some domestic Cheddars have is thought to be the result of pasteurization, or of what the cows feed on—silage in winter, bitter herbs or grasses in spring and summer. It's always best, if you can, to sample Cheddar before buying.

Cheddars labeled *mild* are aged two to three months; *mellow* indicates over four months; *sharp* means six to twelve months. Most pre-packaged supermarket cheeses receive minimum aging, although some are good values. Older Cheddars, those aged over a year, usually have the greatest character and flavor, but they are also scarcer and more expensive. They also keep the best. Uncut wheels of Cheddar keep several months in the refrigerator. Sharp Cheddar also keeps well if cut surfaces are securely protected with plastic wrap or foil. The color of Cheddar has nothing to do with its taste. Cheddars range in hue from almost white to pale yellow to bright pumpkin orange, usually determined by regional custom or preference. Vermont purists like their Cheddar white (yellow is also made), while in Wisconsin the preference is for deep orange-gold. Natural vegetable dye from the Latin American annatto bean is used to give color.

Mature Cheddar is excellent with apples, grapes, or other fresh fruit and with well-aged red wines such as Bordeaux or Cabernet Sauvignon. Cheddar is widely produced in the United States and some of the best have local identities or special names:

COON CHEDDAR:

One of the sharpest American Cheddars, usually aged a year or more, Coon is crumbly-textured and darker in color than most because of the patented method of curing it at higher temperatures.

GOAT'S MILK CHEDDAR:

A white Cheddar made in Iowa. Goat's milk Cheddar is not like other Cheddars, but has the rich and faintly sweet character of goat's milk. Not widely available.

NEW YORK CHEDDAR:

One of the finest raw-milk Cheddars. *Herkimer* is white and sharp with excellent character and depth of flavor; its name should be specifically marked on it. *Cooper Cheddar* is another New York variety, a little mellower and softer than Herkimer, crumbly in texture, and yellow in color. Smoked Cheddar is also produced in New York.

PINEAPPLE CHEDDAR:

A cheese first made in Litchfield County, Connecticut, Pineapple Cheddar got its name from the way it was suspended in netting during the curing process. The crisscross, diamond-shaped impressions on the rind resembled the exterior of a pineapple; it was also pineapple-shaped. Rarely seen now.

TILLAMOOK CHEDDAR:

Yellow Cheddar from Oregon made exclusively from raw milk. It ranges from very mild to sharp. Well-aged Tillamook is highly prized by Oregonians but is generally available only on the West Coast and in a few specialty cheese shops elsewhere in the United States.

VERMONT CHEDDAR:

Consistently one of America's best and most distinctive Cheddars, Vermont is rich, but sharp and assertive. It is usually the color of sweet butter but is sometimes yellow-orange or tinged with faint gold. *Crowley* is a Vermont original, a granular-curd Cheddar made by the Crowley family. It is more open-textured, softer, and has a higher moisture content than other Cheddars and becomes quite tangy with a year's aging. VERMONT SAGE is Cheddar flavored with sage.

WISCONSIN CHEDDAR:

Cheddars from Wisconsin are produced in greater quantities than other American Cheddars and range from fair to very good in quality. *Colby,* named for the town in Wisconsin where it was created, is a mellow, soft-textured, Cheddar-style cheese made by the washed-curd process that eliminates the step of "cheddaring;" *Longhorn* is the name of another, usually mild, Wisconsin Cheddar. Smoked and flavored Cheddars are also produced in quantity in Wisconsin.

The Big Cheese

The world's largest cheeses have been Cheddars. Queen Victoria was the honored recipient of one of the earliest mammoth Cheddars—a bridal gift that weighed in at about a ton. But it has been the North American cheese-makers who have produced the behemoths of cheese. A fourteen-hundred-pound Cheddar was given to Andrew Jackson in the White House. A four-ton Cheddar was displayed at the Toronto World's Fair in 1883. In 1937, a six-ton Cheddar graced the New York World's Fair. But this hefty fellow was dwarfed by a seventeen-ton giant displayed at the 1964 World's Fair in Flushing Meadow, New York. Largest in the world to date, the '64 Cheddar was made by fifteen Wisconsin and Canadian cheese-makers. It was subsequently displayed in England and eventually purchased by a London restaurant, where it was served with great ceremony.

CHEDDAR, CANADIAN

ORIGIN	*Canada/cow's milk*
TYPE	*semi-firm, Cheddar/45% fat*
TASTE	*savory to sharp*
APPEARANCE	*pale yellow, firm, close-textured interior; natural or black waxed rind*
AVAILABILITY	*general export*

Canadian Cheddars as a group are of superior quality, and the best of them are surpassed only by genuine English farm-house Cheddars. Two of the most respected brands are Black Diamond and Cherry Hill. Black Diamond, some of which is aged up to 30 months, is dependably excellent, a pale gold cheese of great character, a rich, satisfying texture, and fine aftertaste. Among American Cheddars, it is the best buy as an after-dinner cheese accompanied by fresh fruit and a mature red wine, such as Cabernet Sauvignon.

CHEVREESE

ORIGIN	*New Jersey/goat's milk*
TYPE	*fresh/45% fat*
TASTE	*fresh, acid, lactic, with a clean finish*
APPEARANCE	*soft, white interior like whipped Cottage Cheese; sold in plastic containers*
AVAILABILITY	*local only*

This pot-style goat cheese has an appealing tartness, lactic, rather acidic, flavors, and a wholesome, brisk aftertaste. It does not have as much individuality of character as older, similar cheeses from Europe, although it has made a promising start. Chevreese is produced by the LeComte family in Lebanon, New Jersey, from 100% goat's milk.

COLBY *see also* Cheddar, American

A softer Cheddar named for the Wisconsin town where it was first made. Higher in moisture content and aged for only a month or so, it doesn't keep as well as other Cheddars but is very popular as a snack or a sandwich cheese.

COLDPACK CHEESE

This popular specialty consists of two Cheddars ground together, sometimes with flavorings. The mixture is not heated and coldpack is therefore not a processed cheese. One of the most popular, and one of the best, Coldpack cheeses is Port Wine Cheddar, a soft, spreading cheese with a touch of sweetness from the addition of domestic port wine. A savory and tangy snack or appetizer, served on crackers, Melba toast, or dark breads, it is sold in small containers or crocks of various sizes.

COON CHEDDAR *see* Cheddar, American

COTTAGE CHEESE

ORIGIN	*U.S.A., Canada/cow's milk*
TYPE	*fresh/4–8% fat*
TASTE	*smooth and bland or tangy*
APPEARANCE	*loose or dense snowy white curds, in containers*
AVAILABILITY	*domestic*

The curds of American Cottage Cheese are usually washed to cut the acidity, which makes it milder than the many acid-curd fresh cheeses produced abroad. An acid-curd Cottage Cheese is made in the United States, but sweet curd is far more common. Creamed Cottage Cheese has four to eight percent cream mixed with it. Brands vary in the size and density of the curds; "California-style" tends to have small curds, densely packed. Pot-style is usually whipped.

The life of Cottage Cheese is brief, so the fresher, the better. The best guide to freshness is the "pull date," or date after which it should not be sold, that is printed on the carton. Best known as a diet food, Cottage Cheese is full of minerals and enzymes. It goes with a variety of fruits and is quite good with black coffee.

CREAM CHEESE

ORIGIN *U.S.A., Canada/cow's milk*
TYPE *fresh/35% fat*
TASTE *fresh, creamy, appealingly sour*
APPEARANCE *snow-white bricks, foil-wrapped or whipped, in waxed containers*
AVAILABILITY *domestic*

Good Cream Cheese can be a singularly satisfying spread for sandwiches or bagels. Most contain emulsifiers, such as gum arabic, but the best do not. And the best are fresher, lighter, and more flavorful, but are also more open-textured and have a somewhat shorter keeping time. Cream Cheese mixed with jam or preserves is a treat; it also combines well with cucumbers, tomatoes, watercress, sliced olives, and, of course, lox and red onions.

Neufchatel, copied after French Neufchatel, has less butterfat and more moisture than regular Cream Cheese. Unlike the French version, it is unripened and often mixed with flavorings such as minced fruit, vegetables, or spices.

FARMER CHEESE

Farmer Cheese is basically Cottage Cheese pressed into a firm mass the shape of a flat brick. Fresh and mild, it is often a breakfast cheese, topped with fruit or salt, pepper, and a dollop or two of sour cream.

GOAT'S MILK CHEDDAR *see* Cheddar, American

HAND CHEESE

An American descendant of German HANDKÄSE, Hand Cheese was developed first in Pennsylvania and later in other German-American communities. Like its German counterpart, it is hand-shaped into small flat discs. It ripens in a yellow to reddish-brown washed rind and becomes creamy-soft, with pungent flavors and aromas. Such cheeses eventually become quite rank, in fact, and should be well-wrapped when stored. They are traditionally accompanied by dark beer.

LIEDERKRANZ

ORIGIN *Ohio/cow's milk*
TYPE *soft-ripened/50% fat*
TASTE *mild to pungent and strong-smelling*
APPEARANCE *foil-wrapped, four-ounce bars; soft ivory interior*
AVAILABILITY *domestic*

Liederkranz is the most famous American original, invented in 1882 by a New York cheese-maker, Emil Frey. Frey was trying to imitate the German SCHLOSSKÄSE, a strong-smelling, soft-ripened cheese similar to Limburger. Frey named it after the Liederkranz Hall singing group in New York, because of their enthusiasm for the cheese.

Liederkranz is a good example of the complexities involved in making fine cheese. When the plant that made it first moved from New York to Van Wert, Ohio, the producers were unable to get the right flavor—even though they had taken precautions to insure that the production procedures remained the same. Somehow they hit upon the idea of smearing the walls with cheeses made in New York—Eureka! The air-borne bacteria from other New York cheeses had subtly affected the flavor of Liederkranz as it ripened.

Liederkranz is put on the market from four to six weeks from the date that appears on the package. When young, it is mild and semi-soft. As it matures in its foil-wrapped packaging, it becomes honey-colored, creamy-soft, and progressively stronger in aroma and taste; the rind turns from yellow to golden brown. Though pungent, it is never as strong or smelly as Limburger. When too old, however, it smells rank, even stinky, and feels dried out or sticky. Like other strong-smelling cheeses, it is good with dark bread, green onions, and dark beer.

MAYTAG BLUE *see* Blues

MINNESOTA BLUE *see* Blues

MONTEREY JACK (also California Jack) *see also* Sonoma Jack

ORIGIN *California/cow's milk*
TYPE *semi-soft/50% fat*
TASTE *smooth and bland, Aged Jack sharp and flavorful*
APPEARANCE *very pale yellow to rich orange, depending on age; dark rind cylinders; sold as loaves or wheels*
AVAILABILITY *domestic (Aged Jack mainly California)*

Though Monterey Jack is classified as a Cheddar, young cheeses aged two to three weeks are as mild and pale as young Goudas. Some are blander, to the point of lacking much flavor at all, which is why flavored ones such as

Jalapeno Pepper Jack are so popular. As a high-moisture cheese, young Jack is good as a snack or sandwich cheese; it is often used as topping on Mexican dishes. The name is said to have come from David Jacks, who first marketed the cheese in Monterey County, California.

Quite different from young Jack is Dry or Aged Jack, which may be made from partially skimmed milk. Aged six months or more, it develops a tough brown, wrinkled hide and a firm, rich yellow interior. The aged version resembles Cheddar in texture and flavor, and it's rich, nutty, salty and sharp—excellent with Cabernet Sauvignon or Zinfandel. It is also used for grating.

Jack cheese has become quite popular nationwide and young Jack is produced by several large United States factories. The best, however, is still produced by small companies in California and specialties such as dill-flavored, rennetless versions (for vegetarians) and fine Dry Jack are only available in the West.

MOZZARELLA

The American version of this fresh Italian cheese is made mostly in factories and sold in supermarkets. If not too old (and bitter) it is fine for cooking but not delicate enough to eat fresh. Mozzarellas made in Italian shops, often daily, can be excellent, however, especially when very fresh and dressed with olive oil, salt, and freshly ground pepper. Smoked Mozzarella has a delightful, lightly smoked flavor that makes a delicious snack and a unique garnish for salads.

MÜNSTER (also Muenster)

Widely produced in America and generally reliable in quality, American Münster has a thin orange rind, a pale yellow interior, and resilient texture. Often quite bland, American Münster is never as strong in flavor or aroma as Alsatian MÜNSTER. At its most flavorful, domestic Münster is savory but simple in character. It is good with fruit, beer, or light fruity wines.

NEW YORK CHEDDAR *see* Cheddar, American

OKA

ORIGIN	*Quebec/cow's milk*
TYPE	*semi-soft, monastery/45–50% fat*
TASTE	*smooth, flavorful, piquant*
APPEARANCE	*wheels with rounded sides*
AVAILABILITY	*limited export*

One of the few genuine monastery cheeses in this hemisphere, Oka was originally made at *Fromagerie de la Trappe,* a Trappist monastery in Oka, Quebec, in the latter half of the nineteenth century. In 1975, the monks sold the company to a factory producer in Oka, but the old recipe is still used and the monks still oversee production methods. Highly regarded for its fine character—creamy, full-flavored, becoming stronger as it ripens—it is modeled after French PORT SALUT.

Today's version, aged about 30 days on cypress slats in the aging cellars, is said to lack the deep, penetrating flavors of the longer-ripened original made at the monastery. However, it is still considered one of the better cheeses produced in the Americas and demand usually outstrips supply. It goes well after dinner with full-bodied red wines.

OREGON BLUE *see* Blues

PARMESAN

American versions of Italian PARMESAN are either too salty or too sharp and almost always lacking in flavor. One exception is the Parmesan made by the Stella company in Wisconsin. Though somewhat uneven in quality, it is a cut above other domestic versions and is available in supermarkets. Pregrated Parmesan is always second-rate and bears little resemblance to true Parmesan, as a single experience with Italian PARMIGIANA-REGGIANO will demonstrate.

PINEAPPLE CHEDDAR *see* Cheddar, American

RICHELIEU

ORIGIN	*Canada/cow's milk*
TYPE	*soft-ripened/50% fat*
TASTE	*mild, creamy*
APPEARANCE	*soft Brie-like but loaf or brick-shaped*
AVAILABILITY	*domestic*

Richelieu is a product of scientific research at Canadian universities and took over 20 years to develop. The efforts aimed for a monastery cheese similar to Bel Paese, but the result is more like factory Brie or Camembert. Though not truly notable, it is creamy, mild, and spreadable.

RONDELÉ

An agreeable, though not truly distinctive, American version of the French triple cream BOURSIN. Rondelé is sometimes flavored with herbs and/or ground pepper.

ROUGE ET NOIR

Rouge et Noir is the brand name for American Brie and Camembert made near Petaluma, California, by a small company founded in 1865 by Jefferson Thompson. These cheeses, like other imitations, do not have the rich, penetrating, unique character of the best French originals. Still, they are flavorful cheeses that, when perfectly ripe, have an appealing character of their own. They are very similar to one another, but the Brie has a more robust flavor. Pull dates are printed on the bottom of the package to give the consumer some idea of freshness. The cheeses ripen to full creaminess within three to four weeks of that date. When too old they are dry and hard and smell strongly of ammonia. The company maintains that when fully ripe and creamy throughout, the cheeses will freeze well without the texture changing.

Two other cheeses are also produced: Breakfast Cheese, a small soft-ripening cylinders with savory, dry flavors and a slightly grainy texture; and Schloss, salty, soft-ripened little bricks that are ripened 45 days. Their pungent, garlicky aromas and flavor will appeal to lovers of strong cheeses.

SONOMA JACK

ORIGIN	*California/cow's milk*
TYPE	*semi-soft/45% fat*
TASTE	*mild and smooth, sometimes flavored*
APPEARANCE	*sold in pale yellow bricks or wedges with thin natural rinds, or rindless*
AVAILABILITY	*local only*

This cheese is a high-moisture, semi-soft cheese very similar to Monterey Jack and made in the town of Sonoma, California. Produced in two local, family-owned firms, the cheeses are hand-turned daily while being cured in a brine solution. The cheese is basically mild and bland, but there are several versions flavored with garlic, spices, hot peppers, and other seasonings. It is popular as a snack and sandwich cheese, being of very sliceable texture, but is more limited in distribution than Monterey Jack.

Wheels of Dry Jack, aged several months, are occasionally available. These are superb, firm-textured cheeses with tough, dark brown rinds, a flaky, dry texture similar to Cheddar, and rich, salty flavors. Dry Jack keeps well for many months and is hard enough for grating.

TELEME

A soft cheese similar to domestic Brie, Teleme has a little more bite and tang. Aged about 21 days and hand-turned daily, it has up to 50% butterfat and a creamy consistency. Riper Teleme is runnier in texture and more pronounced in flavor. It is mainly available in northern California.

TILLAMOOK *see also* Cheddar, American

Very good Cheddar made in Tillamook County, Oregon.

VERMONT CHEDDAR *see* Cheddar, American

VERMONT SAGE *see also* Cheddar, American

VERMONT CHEDDAR flavored with sage or sage flavoring. The best are the farm-produced varieties with bits of the herb worked into the curd, but they are made in small quantity and are only available locally.

WISCONSIN CHEDDAR *see* Cheddar, American

SERVING CHEESE

A fine cheese needs no embellishment, yet cheese of any kind is never eaten just by itself. The simpler its accompaniments, however, the better, especially when it occupies center stage—as a lunch, a snack, or a course on its own. Cheese goes with a variety of things, but by time-honored tradition bread, fruit, and wine are its classic companions. Local breads and cheeses often complement one another superbly—the dark breads of Scandinavia, for example, Danish pumpernickel, Swedish limpa, caraway rye, are fine with the semi-soft varieties so prevalent there; crusty french baguettes are unbeatable for Brie, Camembert or other soft-ripened cheeses.

Quite a fuss is made in England over crackers to go with cheeses, according to an English friend of mine. There is heated discussion on the subject, he says, and something of a ritual involved in pairing the right crackers with certain cheeses. For some, it must be hard, large-ish biscuits known as Bath Olivers with Stilton. Others won't do without their tin of Romary's, which are a little sweeter and very good with Cheddar, or Cornish wafers, or Carr's Water Biscuits. Whatever the type of cracker, unsalted ones are best for most cheeses because most are often quite salty already.

What is it about fruit that sets off cheese so superbly? Perhaps it is the refreshing contrast of crisp acidity and juicy sweetness. Few would eschew the pleasures of ripe pears and Gorgonzola, apples with Cheddar or Wensleydale, summer berries with Petit-Suisse or the creams, ripe plums with *chèvres,* or fresh figs with young Parmigiano.

Although cheese is good with ale, beer, cider, and in some instances, strong black coffee, wine most often partners it best. Wine and cheese are boon companions that seem to bring out the best in one another. There is a saying in the wine trade: buy on apples, sell on cheese. The natural acidity of apples points up defects in a wine, but cheese makes any wine taste good. The milky proteins and richness of cheese take the edge off a harsh wine and tame rampant tannins or acidity. Some wine and cheese marriages seem preordained on high so sublime are they: Stilton with Port, Roquefort with Sauternes, ripe Camembert and mature Bordeaux, Dry Jack with Zinfandel.

Cheeses served on home ground are often excellent with the local drink. Never have I enjoyed the goaty tang of *chèvre* more than in the little hilltop town of Sancerre in the Loire Valley, sitting in the sun-dappled square, munching away on a pair of crusty Crottins washed down by the crisp wine that is also called Sancerre.

Cheese is appropriate served at all times of day or night—for breakfast, lunch, dinner, and snacks in between. In parts of Europe, like Holland and Scandinavia, it is commonly a breakfast food. In London, the Ploughman's Lunch of cheese, ale, bread, and sometimes chutney is a pub classic. In America, cheese is most widely used for sandwiches, snacks, or cooking, and most of the cheese products, unfortunately, are suitable for little else, certain well-aged Cheddars being the exception.

Cheese is a popular food for large cocktail parties, where people need more substantial nourishment to sustain them for long periods, or to soak up alcohol. It is ideal for wine tasting (for serious blind tastings, however, the cheese should *follow* the tasting so as not to interfere with fair judgment of the wines).

Cheese increasingly has an important part to play in the principal meal of the day, but because it is so adaptable it is often abused. It is, for example, commonly served as an appetizer with cocktails before dinner. With certain exceptions, this doesn't seem suitable to me. Most cheeses are fairly dense or heavy, sometimes quite cloying, often leaving a sharp aftertaste. Cheeses are so tasty, moreover, that guests may be tempted to eat too much at this stage and spoil their appetites for the meal to come.

Interesting exceptions do exist, however. In Spain, it is customary to serve bits of Manchego and salted nuts with Fino or Dry Oloroso Sherry. Here the body of the fortified wine nicely cuts through the savory richness of the cheese. The Spanish are wise enough not to overdo it, serving only a few bits of cheese before going into dinner. Other exceptions for before dinner are fresh double creams such as Boursin or creamy blues such as Blue Costello or Gorgonzola Dolcelatte, which can be spread on light wafers. These may be quite acceptable with the ubiquitous glass of white wine that is so boringly popular now, or with the best aperitif of all—Champagne.

Cheese and Beverage Pairings

CHEESE	TYPE
Appenzeller, Blarney, Beaufort, Emmental, Gruyère, Jarlsberg, Samsoe (Swiss types)	Swiss
Beer Cheese, Bierkäse, American Brick, German Tilsit	Monastery
Bel Paese, Saint-Paulin, Port-Salut, Saint-Nectaire, Tourton	Semi-soft
Blues, creamy blues	Blue vein
Brie, Camembert, Paglietta	Soft-ripened
Cheddar, Cheshire, Double Gloucester, Dunlop	Semi-firm
Chèvres, Feta	Goat
Crema Dania, Chaource, Explorateur, Corolle, Saint-André, Boursault, Vacherin Mont-d'Or	Soft
Esrom, Fontina, Port-Salut, Taleggio, Tilsit	Semi-soft
Gouda, Harvarti, Danish Muenster, California Jack, Tomme des Pyrénées	Semi-soft
Liederkranz, Limburger, Hervé, Handkäse	Monastery
Parmesan, Grana, Sbrinz, Asiago, Fiore Sardo	Hard
Pont l'Evêque, Chaumes, Maroilles, Rollet, Vieux Pané, Taleggio di Monte, Livarot	Surface-ripened
Provolone, Scamorze, Mozzarella	Pasta-filata
Aged Gouda, Dry Monterey Jack	Hard

To my mind, the best time for cheese is after dinner, as a course of its own. At formal dinners and the best restaurants, cheese is served as a separate course following the entrée or salad and preceding dessert and coffee. In France it is sometimes served at the same moment as the salad. This is fine, certainly, but since I generally want wine with cheese, I prefer to serve the salad first and then the cheese. Cheese can also serve *as* dessert. People are eating more lightly today, so the cheese course sometimes serves as dessert, accompanied by fresh fruit.

Selections for an after-dinner cheese board should include cheeses with a variety of flavors and textures, ranging from mild to assertive, soft to firm, young and fresh to more mature. There should be at least one mild and popular cheese for the less adventurous or inexperienced, and a variety of shapes and colors that make a visually attractive presentation. You don't want to serve several semi-soft or firm cheeses, or all blues or *chèvres* (unless the group is into tasting the fine subtleties among them). Remember that strong-smelling cheeses like Livarot, Limburger, Handkäse, or ripe Münster will overpower more delicate ones, so place them well apart and provide separate serving knives for them.

BEVERAGE

Fruity reds, Beaujolais, Chinon, Barbera, Gamay, Zinfandel, Chelois

Beer or full-bodied reds, Petite Sirah, Dão, Zinfandel

Fruity whites or reds, Chenin Blanc, Napa Gamay, Beaujolais, Côte du Rhône

Full-bodied reds, Sauternes or Port, Barolo, Hermitage, Nuits-St.-Georges, Chambertin, Shiraz, Riesling, Mâcon Blanc, Champagne

Mature reds, Bordeaux, Cabernet Sauvignon, Burgundy, Pinot Noir

Mature, balanced reds, Bordeaux, Burgundy, Ruby Port, bitter beer

Crisp dry whites, fruity or mature reds, Retsina, Sancerre, Sauvignon Blanc, Chardonnay, Cabernet Sauvignon, Burgundy, Ruby Port

Dry whites, mature reds or Champagne

Beaujolais, Rhone, light Cabernet, Valpolicella

Light Bordeaux or Cabernet, Beaujolais, Côte du Rhône

Beer or ale

Barolo, Chianti Riserva, Vino Nobile di Montepulciano, Rubesco, Brunello di Montalcino, Taurasi

Assertive, vigorous reds, Saint-Emilion, Hermitage or Côte Rotie, Cabernet or Zinfandel

Chianti, Valpolicella, Cabernet del Trentino

Zinfandel

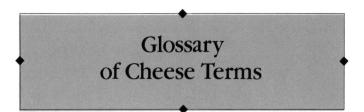

Glossary
of Cheese Terms

Acid, acidity: a description of a pleasant tang; it can be a defect if too PRONOUNCED.

Affiné: from the French *affiner,* meaning "to finish, or refine." WASHED-RIND cheeses, for example, may be *affiné au marc de Bourgogne*—the rind has been washed with *marc* during CURING.

Ammoniated: a term describing cheeses that smell or taste of ammonia, a condition that afflicts the rinds of overripe cheeses, primarily those with bloomy rinds such as Brie, Camembert, CHÈVRES. A hint of ammonia is not necessarily objectionable.

Annatto: a yellow-orange dye extracted from the seeds of a South American plant and used to color such cheeses as Cheddar, Mimolette, Double Gloucester, Edam, and many others.

Aroma: the smell or odor of cheese, which can vary from very faint to over-poweringly STRONG. Aroma is an excellent guide to personal preference in cheeses, though sometimes the smell is stronger than the taste on the palate, as with French Münster, Pont l'Evêque, Liederkranz, where the odor is mainly in the rind.

Assertive: term referring to pronounced taste or aroma.

Barnyardy: a term used to describe aromas or flavors associated with a stable or barnyard. The description is not necessarily negative, but it can refer to an excessively goaty, EARTHY, or even dirty character.

Beestings: a term for colostrum, the first milk a cow gives after calving. Very high in protein, its only known use is in Spain for a strong, semi-firm cheese known as Armada.

Bleu: the French term for "blue."

Bloomy rind: the white fleecy rind that develops on certain surface-ripened cheeses like Brie, Camembert, double or triple creams, and some CHÈVRES. It is formed by spraying the surface of the cheese with spores of *Penicillium candidum* mold (see Pencillium) while it is curing.

Blue vein: cheeses that develop bluish or greenish veins of mold throughout their interior. Veining generally gives cheese an ASSERTIVE and PIQUANT flavor. See p. 6.

Body: the "feel" of a cheese, on the palate or to the touch; it may be firm, SUPPLE, SPRINGY, elastic, chewy, GRAINY, etc.

Brine: a salt-and-water solution in which some cheeses are washed or dipped during curing. (See "Washed rind.")

Brushed: To keep the rinds moist, WASHED-RIND cheeses are "brushed" during curing with various liquids, such as brine, beer, or brandy.

Casein: the principal protein in milk that solidifies it into cheese through the action of RENNET.

Chalky: a positive term, referring either to whitest of white color or smooth, fine-grained texture, primarily for CHÈVRES. Not a reference to taste.

Cheddaring: the process used in making Cheddar, whereby the CURDS are cut, or milled, and repeatedly turned to knit the fibers together.

Chèvres: the French term for goat cheeses. See p. 7.

Close: a term describing a smooth, dense texture with no holes; cheeses with more OPEN texture may have large or small holes.

Cold pack: cheeses ground or mixed together into a soft, spreadable paste without heating or cooking. Port Wine Cheddar is an example.

Cooked: part of the cheese-making process during which the cheese is heated to help solidify the CURD. Most cheeses are heated somewhat, but Cheddar- or Swiss-types are heated to fairly high temperatures.

Creams, Double or Triple: a classification of cheese. See p. 8.

Creamy: a term describing texture or taste. Creamy texture is soft and even runny in some cases; creamy flavors are rich and associated with cream-enriched cheeses such as double or triple creams. Creamy may also describe a cream-colored appearance of the PASTE.

Crumbly: a descriptive term for texture that may be positive or not, depending on whether it is typical of the cheese. Blues may be somewhat crumbly, but if they are too much so, they are dried out.

Cryovac: vacuum-plastic wrapping commonly used for cheese portions sold in supermarkets. Large factory-made cheeses are sometimes cryovacked also. This method of packaging has the advantage of protecting the cheese from oxidation or spoilage, but it can result in GUMMY rinds and mushy texture, particularly with blue cheeses.

Curd: the solid white mass that coagulates when milk is treated with RENNET or other acid-producing enzymes, leaving the WHEY.

Curing: the process of ripening that natural cheeses undergo to achieve peak flavor; often used interchangeably with *aging* or *ripening.*

Dry matter: all the components of cheese excluding moisture (water). They include proteins, milk fat, milk sugars, and minerals.

Earthy: a term describing hearty, RUSTIC flavors and certain cheeses with ASSERTIVE flavor or aroma, particularly monastery types but also sheep or goat cheeses. It is not negative unless excessive.

Eyes: the holes found in some cheeses, especially Swiss or Gruyères. Eyes are formed by gases that are released during the CURING process.

Fat content: The fat content of a cheese is measured only in the DRY MATTER, because moisture content varies as the cheese gets older. Fat content for most cheeses is 45% to 50% of the dry matter; a few have only 10% or less, double creams have 60%, triple creams have 75%.

Ferme, or **Fermier:** the French term for farm-produced cheeses.

Fresh: a classification of cheese. See p. 9.

Formaggio: Italian word for cheese.

Fromage: French word for cheese.

Fruity: a descriptive term for the sweet and appealing fragrance or flavor of certain cheeses, common to some of the monastery types or semi-firm mountain cheeses.

Gamy: a descriptive term for STRONG cheeses with penetrating aromas.

Gassy: a descriptive term for defective cheeses that have gassy or fermented ordors.

Goat: a classification of cheese. See p. 7.

Grainy: a term used for describing gritty texture, desirable in certain hard, grating cheeses though not to the point of mealiness. Unless it is typical of the cheese, graininess is an undesirable trait.

Grana: Italian term for hard, grating cheeses like Parmigiano-Reggiano, Grana Padano, Sapsago, etc. See p. 3.

Gummy: a negative term used to describe an overly plastic texture, as well as overripe rinds that have become sticky or gooey. Gumminess is undesirable in any context.

Hard: a classification of cheese. See p. 3.

High: a descriptive term sometimes applied to strong-smelling cheeses that have reached full ripeness or are just over the edge.

Interior: the part of the cheese inside the rind or crust; also called PASTE.

Kaas: the Dutch word for cheese.

Käse: the German word for cheese.

Lactic: a generally positive description applied to cheeses with a clean, wholesome, milky flavor.

Lait cru: French term for raw milk.

Laiterie or laitier: French words for dairy or dairyman; appears on French cheeses made in creamery or factory. (See "Ferme.")

Marc: white brandy or *eau de vie* made from grape pomace; sometimes used as the solution for curing WASHED-RIND cheeses.

Matieres grasses: the French term for DRY MATTER.

Mild: a descriptive term for cheeses that have bland or unassuming flavor; also a term for young Cheddars that are aged briefly.

Mold: a condition created by the spores of various fungi during ripening that also contributes to individual character. Surface molds ripen from the rind inward; internal molds (such as those used for blue cheeses) ripen from the interior outward. A *moldy* character can be clean and attractive or unpleasantly ammoniated. *Mold* also refers to the fungus itself.

Monastery: a classification of cheese. See p. 4.

Mushroomy: a descriptive term commonly applied to some soft-ripened cheeses that have developed the pleasant aroma of mushrooms.

Natural rind: rinds that develop naturally on the cheese's exterior during ripening, without the aid of ripening agents or washing. Most semi-firm or hard cheeses have natural rinds that may be thin like Cheddar or tough and thick like Parmesan, Pecorino Romano, Swiss Emmentaler and others.

Nutty: a term used to describe flavors reminiscent of nuts, often hazelnuts or walnuts.

Oily: a term used to describe the texture of some semi-firm or hard cheeses; it can also apply to aroma and flavor.

Open: open-textured cheeses are those that have holes. They may be small or large, densely patterned, or randomly scattered and irregular in shape (see "Close").

Ost: the Scandinavian term for cheese.

Paraffin: the wax coating applied to the rinds of some cheeses, intended to protect them during export and add to their lifespans. The coating may be clear, black, yellow, or red.

Pasta filata: Italian term for cheeses whose curds are dipped in hot whey, then kneaded or stretched to an elastic consistency. (See p. 8.)

Pasteurized: a term describing milk that has been heat-treated to destroy bacteria. Most factory-made cheeses are made from pasteurized milk to ensure greater control over quality and more uniform consistency. Processed cheeses may also be pasteurized to check further ripening.

Paste: a term for the interior of a cheese, most commonly used with soft-ripening varieties that are semi-soft to runny.

Penicillium: principal species of fungi used to develop molds on certain cheeses during ripening. *Penicillium candidum* is used to develop many soft-ripened cheeses, such as Brie; *Penicillium glaucum* or *roqueforti* is used for blue cheeses.

Persillé: French word meaning "parsleyed;" applied to delicately veined blues where the MOLD resembles sprigs of parsley.

Pickled: a term sometimes used for cheeses cured in BRINE, such as Feta.

Piquant: a term used to describe an appealing sharpness or exhilarating accent of flavor or aroma.

Processed: a classification of cheese. See p. 10.

Pronounced: a descriptive term for forceful aroma or flavor.

Pungent: strong, sharp, penetrating aroma or flavor.

Queso: Spanish word for cheese.

Rancid: a term referring to stale, fetid, or otherwise tainted character.

Rennet: a substance, found in the mucous membranes of calves' stomachs, that contains rennin, an acid-producing enzyme that aids in coagulating milk, or separating the curds from the whey.

Rind: a cheese's outer surface, which varies considerably in texture, thickness, and color. Some cheeses are rindless, some have natural rinds, others possess rinds that are produced by MOLD (BLOOMY RIND).

Ripe: a specific term referring to cheeses that have arrived at peak flavor through aging. The optimum period of aging varies widely with the type of cheese.

Robust: descriptive term for earthy, full-flavored cheeses.

Rubbery: generally a pejorative term for cheeses that are overly chewy or elastic in texture.

Rustic: generally ascribed to country or mountain cheeses that have hearty or earthy flavors and assertive or barnyardy aromas.

Salty: most cheeses have some degree of saltiness; those lacking in salt are said to be dull or flat. Pronounced saltiness is characteristic of some cheeses, but oversaltiness is a defect.

Semi-firm: a classification of cheese. See p. 4.

Semi-soft: a classification of cheese. See p. 4.

Sharp: a term applied to fully developed flavor in aged cheeses like Cheddar, Provolone, and certain blues. If a cheese is too sharp, however, it has become bitter or biting.

Sheep: a classification of cheese. See p. 7.

Soft-ripened: a classification of cheese. See p. 5.

Sour: a mild, sourish tang can be attractive in young cheeses like Stracchino, but this term usually refers to excessive ACIDITY, which is very unpleasant.

Spicy: a descriptive term for cheeses with peppery or herby character. It has a different meaning than *spiced,* which refers to cheeses flavored with herbs or spices like caraway, cumin, pepper, chives, etc.

Springy: a descriptive term for resilient texture that "springs back" when you gently press it. Ripe or nearly ripe soft-ripened varieties should be springy.

Starter: the culture of milk bacteria used to increase lactic acid and to begin the process of flavor development. Starters are carefully selected or cultured by conscientious cheese producers; they are very important in determining the cheese's ultimate character.

Strong: a descriptive term for cheeses with PRONOUNCED or penetrating flavor and aroma. See strong-smelling, p. 9.

Supple: a term used to describe the resilient or pliable texture usually characteristic of semi-soft cheeses. It implies just the right degree of elasticity—the cheese is bendable but not rubbery.

Surface-ripened: a term referring to cheeses that ripen, from the outside in, as a result of the application of MOLD, yeast, or bacteria to the surface. Bloomy rind and WASHED-RIND cheeses are surface-ripened.

Tangy: a generally positive descriptive term that refers to a pleasing acidity or tartness, a thrust of flavor common to CHÈVRES and certain blues.

Texture: the "fabric" or "feel" of cheese, which may be smooth, GRAINY, OPEN or CLOSE, CREAMY, flaky, dense, CRUMBLY, etc., according to the specific variety.

Turophile: the Greek term for one who loves cheese.

Washed rind: a term used to refer to SURFACE-RIPENED cheeses such as Pont l'Eveque, Chaumes, Rollot, whose rinds are washed or BRUSHED with brine, beer, brandy, or other solutions during the curing process. The washing promotes the growth of a reddish-orange bacterial "smear," which contributes to aroma and flavor. See p. 5.

Weeping: a term that describes holes or eyes that are shiny with butterfat. Weeping is a sign of maturity in Swiss-type cheeses such as Emmentaler, Gruyere, Jarlsberg, and others.

Whey: the watery, yellowish liquid that is separated from the coagulated CURDS as the first step in cheese-making. Some cheeses, such as Ricotta or Gjetost, are made from the whey. See p. 10.

INDEX OF CHEESES

◆◆◆

◆

A Directory of
Fine Cheese Shops

Avon
   The Cheese Shop
   802 Fishponds Road
   Bristol

Berkshire
   E P Spackman
   25 High Street
   Hungerford

   Wells Stores
   Streatley
   Reading

Cheshire
   George Dulton & Son Ltd.
   Godstall Lane
   Saint Werburgh Street
   Chester

Cornwall
   The Real Ale
      & Cheese Shop
   9 New Bridge Street
   Truro

Devon
   N H Creber Ltd.
   48 Brook Street
   Tavistock

   Dartington Farm
      Food Shop
   Cider Press Centre
   Shinners Bridge
   Totnes

Hertfordshire
   Cheese Plus
   116 Darkes Lane
   Potters Bar

Lancashire
   Bambers Cheese Shop
   13 Orchard Street
   Preston

Leicestershire
   The Cheese Shop
   17 Church Street
   Market Harborough

   Farmhouse Cheese &
      Farmhouse Mill
   55–56 King Street
   Melton Mowbray

   David North Ltd.
   289 Station Road
   Rothley

Lincolnshire
   The Cheese Shoppe
   25 Market Place
   Spalding

London
   Bartholdi
   4 Charlotte Street, W1

   The Common Wine
   14 Bellevue Road, SW17

   A Cordeau & Son Ltd.
   32 Streatham High Road
   SW16

   Delicatessen Shop
   23 South End Road, NW3

   Fortnum & Mason
   181 Piccadilly, W1

   Harrods
   Brompton Road, SW1

   Mainly English
   14 Buckingham Palace Road
   SW1

   Osio & Gioberti
   62–64 High Road, N2

Paxton & Whitfield
93 Jermyn Street, SW1

Rosslyn Delicatessen
56 Rosslyn Hill, NW3

Selfridges
Oxford Street, W1

Lothian
Choosa Cheese
178 Bruntsfield Place
Edinburgh

R W Forsyth Ltd.
30 Princes Street
Edinburgh

Manchester
The Cheesery
1 Regent Road
Altrincham

Merseyside
Fashoni's Cheese Centre
The Market
Southport

Somerset
Chewton Cheese Dairy
Priory Farm
Chewton Mendip

Suffolk
The Cheese Shop
74 Beccles Road
Oulton Broad

Surrey
Mrs Graham's Delicatessen
14 Red Lion Street
Richmond

Sussex
The Cheeseboard
58 High Street
Hastings

The Cheese Shop
17 Kensington Gardens
Brighton

Yorkshire
Farnley Shop
Farnley Lane
Otley

Powells of Ilkley
19 The Grove Promenade
Ilkley

Reginald P Bush
495 Glossop Road
Sheffield

ACKNOWLEDGMENTS

I wish especially to thank my editor, John Smallwood, and Bill Logan for his help with research and the charts in the book.

Numerous people in the cheese trade were helpful to me in preparing *The Pocket Guide to Cheese*. I wish particularly to express my gratitude to Helen Allen of The Wine and Cheese Center in San Francisco, William Hyde of Balducci's and Giorgio DeLuca of Dean & DeLuca in New York City. Others who provided special help and expertise included the following:

Richard Allen, The Wine & Cheese Center, San Francisco, Ca.
Amazon Coffee & Tea Co., Inc., New York, N.Y.
Austrian Trade Commission, New York, N.Y.
Hans Bogge, Nyborg & Nelson, New York, N.Y.
British Trade Information Office, New York, N.Y.
John Ciano, Crystal Food Import Corp., Boston, Ma.
DiPalo Dairy Foods, New York, N.Y.
Domestic Cheese Corp., San Francisco, Ca.
Don Epstein, Robin Packing Co., New York, N.Y.
Stephen Fass, Macy's, New York, N.Y.
Heinz Höfer, Switzerland Cheese Association
Holland Cheese Exporters Association
Douglas Johnstone, Marin French Cheese Co., Petaluma, Ca.
Murray Klein, Zabar's, New York, N.Y.
George Lang, New York, N.Y.
Mary Lyons, Food and Wines from France, New York, N.Y.
Milk Marketing Board, Surrey, England
Fritz Maytag, Napa Valley, Ca.
Rosemary Miller, New York, N.Y.
Monterey Cheese Company, San Francisco, Ca.
Yvon Moller, Denmark Cheese Association, Elmsford, N.Y.
New Zealand Milk Products, Inc., Rosemont, Ill.
Thomas B. Phiebig, Galaxy Trading Company, Englewood Cliffs, N.J.
Otto Roth & Co., Moonachie, N.J.
Sonoma Cheese Factory, Sonoma, Ca.
Stephen Spector, Le Plaisir, New York, N.Y.
Switzerland Cheese Association
The Farmhouse English Cheese Federations, London, England
Janet Trefethen, Napa Valley, Ca.
Oulton Wade, J.P., Chester, England
Wisconsin Cheese Makers Association, Madison, Wisc.
Olga Domingez, Zabar's New York, N.Y.